FELLOW OF THE CRAFT

יהוה

FELLOW OF THE CRAFT

By Wisdom a House is Built

A
TREATISE
ON THE
SECOND DEGREE
OF
FREEMASONRY

by
A Brother of the Hermetic Art
❖ *Gregory* ❖ *B.* ❖ *Stewart* ❖

A.L. 6015

Other books by the author:
> *What is Freemasonry, ebook (online)*
> *Masonic Traveler - Essays and Commentary (print)*
> *Masonic Traveler, FreemasonInformation.com (online)*
> *The Apprentice - The World and the Universe As One*

Coming Soon:
> *Master Mason (2016)*

Fellow of the Craft

By Wisdom a House is Built
A Treatise on the Second Degree of Freemasonry

by Gregory B. Stewart

Copyright ©2015, FmI Publishing
ISBN-10:0986204110
ISBN-13:978-0-9862041-1-1
Library of Congress PCN 2015917426

First Printing

Published by FmI Publishing
P.O. Box 14204
Los Angeles, CA 91409

www.FreemasonInformation.com
email: masonictraveler@gmail.com

Questions, comments, inquiries - please send correspondence to the email or address above.

Art, Text and Design by
Gregory Stewart, 2011-2015

Dedicated
to
Those in Pursuit
of the
Hermetic Art

∴ L ∴ V ∴ X ∴

Thank you to the following people who without their support this book would not have been published:

Donald MacCormick, Gord Echlin, Bro. N. S. Jack Ruby, James T. Dean Jr., Bill Schmidt, Chris Davis - Corinthian Lodge, No. 230, A. F. & A. M.; Corey Hilton, Jonathan Carr, Mark J. Robson, David Pearson - Kirkland Lodge, No. 150, F. & A. M., Washington and Liberal Art Lodge, No. 677, F. & A. M., California; Andrew Chellinsky, Adam C. Marks; Monte Harris - Brubaker Lodge, No. 675, Davenport, IA; Bro. Jeffery James; A. H. Dusty Parsons - Kingsport Lodge, No. 688; Gar Pickering, Jeffrey S. Kupperman, Nicholas Vettese - St. John's Lodge, No. 115, Philadelphia; Johnny Arias, 32°, South Pasadena Masonic Temple, No. 290, Southern California Research Lodge; Jeff Ewing, John D. Sprekels Lodge, No. 657; John Merrick; Carlos A. Rodriguez, Saint Cloud Lodge, No. 221, Royal Knights Chapter, Low Twelve Riders MBA; Gary Iverson; Kirk J. Bielskis, Valley of Bay City, A. A. S. R.; Ann Arbor-Fraternity Lodge, No. 262, Free and Accepted Masons, Michigan; Andrew Smith - Lodge of Asaph No. 1319; Thomas Butler, Kelly Feldcamp, Daniel C. Barston; A. C. from Ulster Lodge F. & A. M., No. 193, Saugerties NY; Joseph James; Luis A. Feliciano, Prenna Sergent, Michael M. Garrett; Matt Frye, Glen Burnie Lodge, No. 213, A. F. & A. M.; Randy Milton Reese, Keeth Miller and Eddy Words. A very special thanks to Jorge Dagang.

For D.S.

my

everything...

ILLUSTRATIONS

*Illustrated by the author

CONTENTS

PREFACE

A Struggle Toward the Light.

This work comes at great pains to encapsulate what is a wide and vast field of study into a few words, to better convey understanding. Becoming a Fellow of the Craft is much more than assuming a new title or being promoted into a titular rank - if done properly. The becoming of a Fellow of the Craft is the really the story of becoming a mason.

As tradition goes, the Master degree is seen as the pinnacle of ones initiation. Yet, when examined in conjunction to the lower degrees, its allegorical illustrations seem tangential and almost obtuse when looked at next to its predecessors. The Hiramic legend itself seems to bear no specific relation to the first or second degree except to suggest that this was the same process that the Grand Master himself underwent before assuming his role in the construction of Solomon's Temple. So then, why is there a third degree when the second encapsulates the becoming of a Freemason?

This is a question we need address another time.

In this work, the broad theme is the becoming of a fellow, or more succinctly the becoming a fellow of the craft. That process, in its myriad telling in lodge rooms from time immemorial is the foundation of what makes a man a mason. In more ancient times, the Fellowcraft degree was the pinnacle of Masonry. It was the second and last degree to which brothers would work and grow in their understanding. It was all that was necessary to be a Mason as, once set on the path, the process was a life long journey that continuously built upon itself in quest for mastery. Such is the lesson of this work. Our ultimate goal is to learn, process and assimilate information about ourselves and the world around us for the express goal of increasing our measure of wisdom. It is in that process that we seek to find the liberty that comes from enlightenment. Pike, in Morals and Dogma, calls it our "...struggle toward the Light." The fundamental lesson of receiving the degree of Fellow Craft is to seek that Light. It is in that Light that we find the genius of the divine and the purpose of our being.

Yet, these understandings hold certain universality which are as varied as are the individuals who seek them out. It seems only appropriate to consider that all the mystery schools of wisdom in antiquity and in the modern day strive to impart this lesson. Not the wisdom of divine miracles or blind faith. Rather, they all seek to impart the necessity of understanding and a desire to know more. Perhaps this is the ultimate lesson of the mysteries, that there is no answer other than constant quest to seek the divine in all we do. Ultimately, the quest for wisdom is freedom.

Pike writes "Masonry is a march and a struggle toward the Light. For the individual as well as the nation, Light is Virtue, Manliness, Intelligence, Liberty. Tyranny over the soul or body is darkness. The freest person, like the freest man, is always in danger of re-lapsing into servitude."

Let this be our lesson of the fellow craft, to be such necessitates our freedom from our own mental tyranny.

Greg Stewart
Los Angeles, California
Autumn, A.L. 6015

FREEMASONRY DEFINED

An explanation for those new to the fraternity

Freemasonry is a post-collegiate male fraternity dedicated to the spiritual development of the initiate into a broader sense of the self, how he relates to the Divine, and his contributory role in the world. It conveys this message through a series of progressive degrees initiating the candidate into a deeper level of understanding and membership. Ultimately, the raised Master Mason is given the allegorical tools to further work on and develop his Masonic intuition.

The largest and oldest fraternal order in the world, Freemasonry crosses all religious boundaries to bring together its adherents of all countries, sects, and opinion in peace and harmony to work towards the betterment of all mankind.

DOUBLEHEAD EAGLE

Mackey in his *Encyclopedia of Freemasonry*, quoting from the transactions of *Quatuor Coronati Lodge*, pages 214, volume xxiv, 1911, says of the adoption of the Scottish Rite usage:

"The most ornamental, not to say the most ostentatious feature of the insignia of the Supreme Council, 33 , of the Ancient and Accepted (Scottish) Rite, is the double-headed eagle, surmounted by an imperial crown. This device seems to have been adopted some time after 1755 by the grade known as the Emperors of the East and West; a sufficiently pretentious title. This seems to have been its first appearance in connection with Freemasonry, but history of the high grades has been subjected to such distortion that it is difficult to accept unreservedly any assertion put forward regarding them. From this imperial grade, the double-headed eagle came to the 'Sovereign Prince Masons' of the Rite of Perfection. The Rite of Perfection with its 25 Degrees was amplified in 1801, at Charleston, United States of America, into the Ancient and Accepted Rite of 33, with the double-headed eagle for its most distinctive emblem. When this emblem was first adopted by the high grades it had been in use as a symbol of power for 5000 years, or so. No heraldic bearing, no emblematic device anywhere today can boast such antiquity. It was in use a thousand years before the Exodus from Egypt, and more than 2000 years before the building of King Solomon's Temple."

LODGE of PERFECTION

The Symbolic Lodge and the Ineffable Degrees

The first portion of the Scottish Rite system of degrees is dubbed *The Lodge of Perfection*. This series of degrees includes the 1° through the 14° and are referred to as the ineffable degrees, taken from the Latin *ineffibilis* meaning something that should not be spoken (incapable of being expressed or described in words; inexpressible. Not to be spoken because of its sacredness; unutterable).

FELLOW

A "companion, comrade," c. 1200, from Old English *feolaga* "partner, one who shares with another," from Old Norse *felagi*, from *fe* "money" + lag, from a verbal base denoting "lay." The root sense of *fellow* is "one who puts down money with another in a joint venture."

From the Old English feolaga, "partner, one who shares with another." One of the same kind, one of a pair.

University senses (mid-15c., corresponding to Latin *socius*) evolved from notion of "one of the corporation who constitute a college" and who are paid from its revenues. *Fellow well-met* "boon companion" is from 1580s, hence *hail-fellow-well-met* as a figurative phrase for "on intimate terms."

Online Etymology Dictionary

A member of a learned society.
An incorporated senior member of a college.

Sharing a particular activity, quality, or condition with someone or something.

A participant in a joint venture or corporation.

In the Medical Definition:
A young physician who has completed training as an intern and resident and has been granted a stipend and position allowing him or her to do further study or research in a specialty.

In Masonic Parlance:
An apprentice freemason, who has completed his ritual and degree study, proven his proficiency and achieved an understanding of what it means to BE a Freemason.

*Those passed to being a **Fellow of the Craft** have been found worthy to recieve the rights of further study.*

The teachings of these readings are not
sacramental, so far as they go beyond
the realm of morality into those
of other domains of
Thought and
Truth

THE PATH OF TAV

Invisible, the path before me.
    It does not exist
        Yet, I know that it is.
    A Golden path,
        bright upon the horizon
Marked with the sign of life,
    the Tau cross is my path upon the tree.
I breathe, I move, I feel
    A statement of triune being
        In father, son, and passing.
Yet, without the conjunction of my own will,
    I cease to exist.

Illuminated as if by an unseen lighthouse
    The dark and stormy shoals are
        Illuminated to me
            by long and weary squares
                and ever turning
                    compass marks.
Realization of having come so far brings tears
    Not of wet and weary sorrow,
        But from the awakening that comes from
        Soft spoken words that tell me
            I have never left.

Word and Wisdom are the sons of Genius,
        unforgiving constructs of
                my destructive potential.
                        This is the reason for my journey
So few steps should not feel an eternity,
        the shadow of which
                standing infinitely over the horizon.
What was the unseen blackness of the void,
        is the door to my adytum.
                Open only to those weary travelers
                        found fit for passage under
                                the Pythagorean transom.

The beginning is the end.
        Gouged into the surface of being.
                Invisible, but now seen…
                        seen, but no longer necessary.
The path of Tav on the tree of life has shown me the world
        And the world
                is within
                    myself.

LVX

Illumination
> *Like a blade of light spilling into the void*
> > *Slowing the horrors of the abyss*
> > > *giving them soft shape.*

Super celestial radiance is a gift from our maker
> *In the glow from our sub-lunar subsistence*

Ever increasing, always maturing
> *Hunger driving us on with unquenchable need.*

The edge of the abyss our only impediment
> *Yet, those borders melt with the spearing light.*

We become the illuminated to illuminate.
> *Absolutely knowing*
> > *absolutely nothing.*

We become LVX.

My going-forth is a perpetual instruction.
For Verily the Path of Tav hath its beginning
In the Foundation of Instruction.
Now the burden of the instruction is this:

End and beginning are one.

...what thou seekest,
Truly thou art.

PAUL FOSTER CASE
THE MEDITATION ON TAV
THE BOOK OF TOKENS

...By wisdom a house is built,
and through understanding
it is established...

PROVERBS 24:3
(NIV)

FELLOW OF
THE CRAFT

THE PATH OF TAV
SHITFING CHANGES OF EXISTANCE - THE LvX OF THE UNIVERSE
GREGORY STEWART, PEN & INK ON BOARD
2015

FELLOW OF
THE CRAFT

Intelligence to understand, Honesty to guide intelligence,
Courage to act, Prudence to guide courage, and Love to humanity
composed of the four others....

Second Degree, Scottish Rite Blue Lodge

The second degree of Freemasonry is our enigma. Having undertaken the ritual and trials of the first degree, we now are at a crossroads - we are in one aspect the coalesced form of the Sephirot *Malkuth*, as we discovered in the First Degree, whole and complete yet faced with the next stage of our evolving maturation. It is a progression that necessitates our need to be transformed and given shape for the tasks before us.[1] To do this, we need to study and learn not simply what it means to BE a Freemason but how that practical application addresses the world we move within, the world that is around us and our interactions with the material influences that we encounter. Why we do this, you will recall, is to relate our own elemental being as *Malkuth* to the elemental world in which we have both become and inhabit. As beings in the state of *Malkuth*, the elemental world, we need now traverse upon the path of *Tav*, up the pillar of mercy, furthering our climb in the teachings of the lodge towards becoming a Master. But, this is getting ahead of ourselves. We must first begin our lesson of the Second Degree as a Fellow of the craft with the implementation of our will into manifested action. This is our summation of all things, our end which is without end. The Christian *Volume of the Sacred Law* begins with the utterance of the *Great Architect* in saying, "Let there be light." So too, as light was created, man becomes the blazing starlight in uttering our creative force. To realize that vision, as a traveler, we must climb the steps to achieve a type of gnosis which comes with the achievement of the distinct but unrelated journeys that bind together in an inseparable union. First, our wisdom journey through the three stages of our existence, next the five steps of evolution that take place in our existence, and then the seven steps of knowledge that transform us in the conduct of its predecessors shaping our understanding. Only when we have undergone this journey can we reach the top and acknowledge our being as that of a fellow of the craft as it is there that we find our self - the manmade manifest as he knocks upon the door of illumination. In truth, this is no easy process. Neither is it an external one. As the warning above the temple door admonishes us to *"Know Thyself"* because *"as what you seek you already are."* Little in this journey will change you in an obvious manner. Rather, it is in the subtle shifting of thought that the greatest and most noble developments will occur. This is the middle chamber, the way before the *Holy of Holies*, which is where the need to transform must take place before venturing farther. These ideas seem strange and foreign to how we see our existence within the mun-

FELLOW OF THE CRAFT

dane world, yet they have been in a manner of
practice for millennia in the wisdom schools of
the sacred. What we cannot say, with certainty,
is that these ideas have existed in their present
configuration in the Masonic system, but in a
manner of cause and effect, they have become
a contemporaneous form of this sacred practice
of enlightenment to bring its students from the
earthly state to the celestial so that they may
inhabit the various heavenly apartments above
us in the unfolding universe. This is the *mystic
tie* that binds us - as a fellow of the craft, as a
lodge, as a member of humankind, and as one
can imagine the Great Architect. In this chain
of union, united, the brilliance of the sun illuminates us and the moon and stars sing us the glo-
ries of the divine harmony of Truth. Pike, in his
treatise on the Fellow Craft, writes "Light! All
comes from Light, and all returns to it." Of the
many great lessons of this degree to be learned
this is the most important to understand.

Flush with the transformation of becoming

an Apprentice, we begin the journey to become a fellow and are immediately confronted by a pair of symbolic sentinels guarding our entry through the temple doors into this degree. There, at the sides of the doorway, are the twin stalwart symbolic pillars of *Boaz and Jachin*. Erected in a manner to convey a dramatic effect, these pillars are our first glimpse into the deep well of symbolism in this degree and the lessons that await us over their threshold. But, before we take the steps to move between them, we must first confront the pillars to discern some of the symbolic meaning in their arrangement.

In Masonic tradition, aspirants of this degree are taught that the pillars of Boaz and Jachin represent *science* and *virtue,* which are defined to mean *science as operative masonry* and *virtue as speculative masonry*. While this is encoded in the Masonic ritual, these prescribed meanings of science and virtue are correctly asserted parallels for so great an overall symbol of this degree. Pike, writing in *Morals and Dogma*, agrees

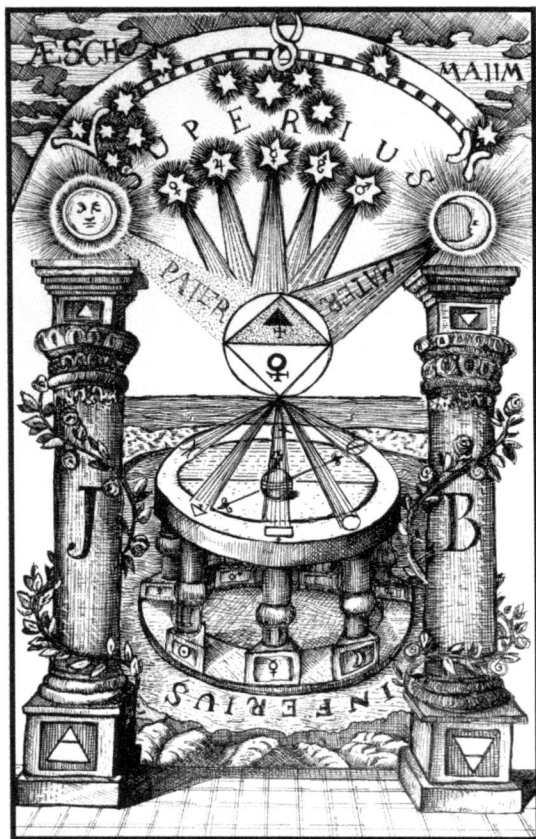

Mystical alchemical diagram of Boaz and Jachin pillars of the Temple of Jerusalem, interpreted as cosmic principles.
Recreated from *The Compass of the Wise (Der Compass der Weisen,* 1782.
Original illustration by Grant Schar
Gregory Stewart, Pen & Ink on Board
2016

as he suggests that there is little value to science taught without virtue, saying "science not teaching moral and spiritual truths is dead and dry." While this is a very terse suggestion, it would seem that Pike is alluding to the symbolic overtones of the pillars themselves, the portico said to be entered into by every advancing Fellow of the Craft. Without laboring too long on these majestic antecedents, we must need look at the parallels of Jachin and Boaz and their correspondence with the Tree of Life.

Through the lens of the Tree, the pillars parallel the left and right pillars of the structure itself. Looking at the pillars, on the right is the pillar of strength, variously said to be the pillar of severity, which corresponds to the pillar of Boaz. On the left is the pillar of Mercy, alternatively called the pillar of wisdom corresponding with Jachin. To see that correspondence, we must look at the allegorical meanings of Boaz and Jachin themselves to gain an understanding of their relationship.

Coming from a Talmudic, and later Old Testament book, Boaz is a major figure in the eighth book of the Bible, *Ruth*, who, as the traditions suggests, is an early ancestor of David and accordingly a prefigurative ancestor of the great teacher Jesus. Interestingly, this also puts the story of Ruth in line with Solomon who, in Masonic telling, is the great patriarch and source of the allegorical temple. In the book of Ruth, Boaz takes the widowed Moabite as his bride because of her goodness. When we look deeper at the story, we learn in the Talmud that Boaz is much more than a man of some stature, being identified as a Judge Ibzan of Bethlehem, marking him as one of the great judges of his people.[2] In that telling, Boaz is portrayed as a just, pious, and learned man who saw a similar piousness in Ruth, conferring with the oracles that she would be the progenitor to a great line of people, ultimately in what would become the line of David. It is because of these qualities of lawfulness and piousness that Boaz wed her, giving her a home and security when others of his people ostracized her as an outsider and foreigner. In looking at its symbolic undercurrents, we can see how this model of strength and severity could be representative of the Talmudic and biblical figure of Boaz and why he would be relatable as the pillar of strength. Ruth, in many ways, represents the acceptance of the outsider to the customary practice and traditional teachings, saying to Naomi:

> *"Where ever you go, I will go!*
> *Where ever you lodge, I will lodge.*
> *Your people will be my people,*
> *and your god, my god."*

Boaz, seeing Ruth's piousness to Jewish Law, discerning through the oracles of his time that Ruth would become ancestress of future kings and prophets. Perhaps Boaz, a man already in his elder years, saw their wise observation of Ruth and believed in the promise and gifts that she would bestow to the tradition of his heritage he held so close.[3]

Correlating the pillar of Jachin is a bit more troublesome, as there is very little on the name in the Judeo/Christian tradition. We can find some resonance when we look at the Hebrew meaning of the word as a name, which is said to be "founding" or "Established by God."[4] In the traditional Masonic ritual, the pillar of Jachin is said to denote establishment which we can see in the scriptural prayer "In strength shall this, my house, be established." This passage, by itself is elusive but may refer to the 24th *Proverb* which reads in the third and fourth passage:

> *By wisdom a house is built,*
> *and through understanding it is established;*
> *through knowledge its rooms are filled with rare*
> *and beautiful treasures.*

If such is the case, then certainly Jachin is a pillar of the degree as it suggests a foundational tradition of establishing wisdom.

One interesting possibility is that the symbolism of Jacin is a misinterpretation of another Christian figure, that of Joachim, the husband of the Catholic Saint Anne, who were together the parents of Mary, the Virgin mother of Jesus. Joachim's story is told in the apocryphal text of the *Gospel of James*, unnamed in the accepted Biblical texts. Joachim, in this context, is said to have been a rich and pious man who gave to the poor. The name Joachim in Hebrew means (יהויקים) God prepares, God will establish." Or, more literally "he whom Yahweh has set up."

Interpreting Jachin in this way is dismissive to the notion of the pillar on the porch of Solomon's Temple but, as throughout this allegorical system Joachim, the grandfather of the Christ, is a pillar in the lineage of Jesus and, like Boaz, a descendant in the house of David. This gives us a pantheon of sorts in the lineage of Solomon – Boaz the antecedent and Jachin (Joachim) a descendant from the line of Solomon. One correspondence that gives this view some merit is the consideration that the pillars of Boaz and Jachin in the original temple were merely names attributed to them as family or craftsman names as some texts have suggested. If taken as the former, they certainly become stalwart symbols of the house of Solomon.

This may be the best encapsulation of the pillars of Boaz and Jachin - wisdom from the knowledge of Jachin, and establishment through the strength as demonstrated by Boaz. One final point to touch on with the pillars is their decoration, which in the Scottish Rite degree are said to encompass the symbolism of the zodiac, the months, the seasons, the elementary points of geometry, unity, peace, plenty, and are topped with two globes, one of the terrestrial earth and the other of the celestial universe, which is said to represent the universality between earth and the heavens of Masonry. As a precursor, the pillars give us a myriad of elements to consider, but as with the degree, they are rather a foreshadowing of the lessons to come. In a less esoteric sense, yet still symbolic, the reference to the pillars is, essentially, an allegorical link to the entering into the temple itself, that their exterior decorations are, essentially, that – mere decorations by which to improve the look of them in such a prestigious presentation of prominence. In one sense, the pillar naming may be simply a convention of attribution, as mentioned above, naming them after patrons of their construction giving them a double role of patronage and religiosity.[5] None-the-less important, the aspirant at the temple door passes over their threshold and into the sacred space of the allegorical temple and into this degree. With these ideas of the pillars coalesced, we can now begin to travel between them and over the threshold to look at the teachings they welcome us into.

It is at this point through the pillars that the aspirant Fellow of the Craft is introduced to the three, five, and seven steps which lead towards the inner recesses of the temple and the doors to the inner sanctum. Before we can approach the door we must first delve deep into the steps but to do that we need first to understand the Kabalistic relationship of the degree and its placement upon the Tree of Life.

In exploring the first degree, we identified its correspondence with the Sephirot of Malkuth. Here, the second degree follows that path upon the Tree of Life taking us to the next step onto the path of Tav, which is, in traditional and esoteric teachings, the 22nd path joining together Malkuth to Yesod. In this Scottish Rite working, traveling the tree of life from the bottom up, the journey on this path is an ascent rather than a descent as we move into its higher teachings. Some interesting aspects to the path of Tav is its origin from antiquity.

In ancient times the symbol *Tav* was the Tau Cross and was representative to life and resurrection used later in Biblical times as a mark on men who lamented sin.[6] This cross is also attributed as the Egyptian cross as the symbol "placed

CRUCIFIED SERPENT - TAU CROSS
RECREATED FROM *R. ABRAHAMI ELEAZARIS URALTES CHYMISCHES WERK.*
SCHWARTZBURGICUM, P. M. & I. P. E. LEIPZIG, IN LANKISCHENS BUCH-
HANDLUNG, 1760. ORIGINAL ENGRAVING BY NICOLAS FLAMEL
GREGORY STEWART, PEN & INK ON BOARD,
2016

[upon] the lips of kings" initiated into the Egyptian Mysteries.[7] When we look at its Judaic origins we find the letter holds the 22nd position in the alphabet, and is often used in Hebrew as the last letter, in words such as *Emet* (אמת), which means *truth*, and is a word made up of the first, middle, and last letters - therefore, all encompassing. Israel Regardie suggests that the Qaballistic path is a representation of the "lowest dregs of the astral plane" and is "symbolic of the universe 'in Toto' as it is the total of all existing intelligence."[8] This becomes an interesting attribute when you consider the symbol, with its tau cross interpretation of antiquity and its resurrecting capacity, which could be construed to be regenerative of its power. Knowledge and wisdom renew one another, which gives the path a reciprocating motion as we move into it and through it, like the motion of a piston or as a beating heart. For the astral location, this seems to fit with a *Hermetic* world view of the universe, as this is one step above the elemental

earth yet still below the stardecked canopy, symbolic of the journey we take in undergoing this degree. In his work, Regardie suggests the path of Tav is the *Yetziratic* path of "the Administrative Intelligence", which it seems, is Athanasius Kircher's same path of "Perpetual Intelligence" which rules the movement of the sun and moon according to their constitution and causes each to gravitate in its respective orbit.[9, 10] Kirchner's description gives us an interesting point to illustrate the action of the Lodge and the making of a Mason, but also lends itself to the degree as a perpetual cycle of knowledge and wisdom which is the resurrecting force in the Tau cross. Perhaps a better illustration is that of a fountain that pulls from its common pool, projecting itself into the air raining its product back upon itself once it has manifested at its zenith. It is in this regenerative upwelling process that we create within, our Blazing Star emitting a continuously pulsating source of internal light. We can see this, too, in Crowley's *Argenteum Astrum (A ∴.*

A ∴) interpretation of this path which says "motion in the physical world of Malkuth has a way of continuing...such sounds and actions are music and dance to natural rhythms." [11] This is, in effect, the process we pass through in our steps between the pillars. We see this in the subtext of the degree in its very numbering.

Schimmel, in her work *The Mystery of Numbers*, finds the number two in antiquity to be a number of "disunion, the falling apart of the absolute divine unity, and therefore connected with the world of creation."[12] While this does have some bearing, it is that duality that exists to create the circulation into and out of this degree's teaching. She goes on to liken the duality to the world of the Persian mystery poet Rumi, when she says he "compared God's creative word Kun with a twisted rope of two threads (which we call twine)"[13] which is the union of two contrasts. We confirm this same teaching of duality in the Zoroastrian tradition by the contrasting of Ahura Mazda, the god of good and light, and

Ahriman, the god of dark and evil principles. The world, our world, is an intermixing of the two, perhaps expressed most succinctly in the Zen representation of the yen and yang. Or, in a more Masonic symbol, the checkered flooring. This is an interesting duality as even in this degree we find the intermixing of knowledge and ignorance as the two powers that operate in the world.

Schimmel draws an interesting parallel to the Gnostic teachings of Manichaeism where the good principle is tied to the spiritual world and evil to the natural (physical) world where our souls strive to break free of the natural prison of the physical. It is, says Cirlot in his *Dictionary of Symbols*, the connecting link between immortal and mortal... the unvarying or the varying.[14]

He draws parallel to the number two (2) to the mandorla-shaped mountains of megalithic cultures where it is "the focal point of symbolic inversion forcing the crucible of life and comprising the two opposite poles of good and evil, life and death."[15] The number two, Cirlot suggests, is the number associated with the *Magna Mater*[16], which comes from Roman mythology as it is associated to the goddess Cybele whose cultic initiation included a shower of blood as a rebirth or re-energization onto which fits the nature of the Fellowcraft degree as it follows the manifestation in the first degree and now reborn through the pillars of Boaz and Jachin.

Through the pillars and now firmly embedded in the degree, the ritual places the candidate in front of a series of symbolic steps, a representation we explored at the conclusion of the Apprentice degree with Jacob's ladder. Cirlot says the symbolism of the steps embraces the essential ideas of "ascension, graduation, and communication between different vertical levels."[17] This is precisely what we have at hand in this Masonic construct. Divided into three sections, the aspirant is faced with three, five, and seven steps, (ascension, graduation and communication) each with its own significance and allegorical lessons to be understood.

At the base, we are confronted with the first three steps, which are significant in their numeration. The purpose of these steps in the degree are said to represent the three principal stages of man: youth, manhood, and maturity. Conversely, the Scottish Rite degree does not reference the three steps as such, instead linking them to the principal supports of the lodge, which are the *Junior* and *Senior Warden* and the *Worshipful Master*, which is of little meaning to anyone unfamiliar with the composition of the lodge. The Rite degree takes a step further, suggesting that the same three can be linked to the idea of Wisdom, Strength, and Beauty, which it defines in its practice as "Wisdom to contrive, Strength to support, and Beauty to adorn the work of the lodge."[18] This link gives us significant connectivity to the three pillars that anchor the Tree of Life - Strength to the left, Wisdom to the right, and Beauty in the center, giving us a good understanding of the importance of matu-

rity in this configuration. In the traditional telling of the second degree ritual, it illuminates the
steps in the working as the stages of life, alluding to our maturation in their progression.[19] In
youth, (and as an entered apprentice) it says that
we "ought industriously to occupy our minds in
the attainment of useful knowledge." As a Fellow Craft, that "we should apply our knowledge
to the discharge of our respective duties to God,
our neighbors, and ourselves. So that, when
taken together, having done the work of the apprentice and as a fellow craft, as Masters we may
"enjoy the happy reflections consequent of a life
well spent and die in the hope of a glorious immortality."[20]

It should be obvious that this first section
of stairs is dense with meaning, but important
nonetheless to put into context the expected
outcomes upon them. This is for all intents and
purposes our movement into the degree, the
crucible within which the chemical reaction of
life and our transformation in it takes place.

Having traversed the first three, we come to rest at the foot of the next series of five steps, which again comes with its own symbolic resonance. Cirlot likens the number five to the *hieros gamos,* which is signified by the number five as it is the representation of the union of the principle of heaven with that of *Magna Mater.*[21] It also has many physical attributes, such as the pentagram and its unique golden section symmetry,[22] and the four limbs and head of the human form. Five, Cirlot says, is "symbolic of man, health, and love, and of the quintessence acting upon matter."[23] From this footing, the Scottish Rite degree associates the five steps to Intelligence, Honesty, Courage, Prudence, and Love towards humanity. It goes further to identify these attributes as, "Intelligence to understand, Honesty to guide intelligence, Courage to act, Prudence to guide courage, and Love to humanity composed of the four others." This is the essence of the degree system and probably one of the most important lessons to be learned within the de-

Chapiteaux des cinq Ordres avec le Chapiteau Ionique
Moderne

Chapiteau Toscan

Chapiteau Dorique

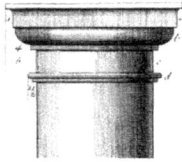

3 Modules ou 24 minutes

Chapiteau Ionique

Chapiteau Ionique Moderne

Chapiteau Corinthien

Chapiteau Composite

3 Modules ou 36 minutes

CLASSICAL ORDERS OF ARCHITECTURE, ENGRAVING FROM THE
ENCYCLOPEDIE VOL. 18. 18TH-CENTURY FRENCH ENGRAVING (CHAPITEAUX
DE FORMES CLASSIQUES. PLANCHE VII (VOL. XVIII) DE L'ENCYCLOPEDIE DE
DIDEROT ET D'ALEMBERT.) ORDERS INCLUDE: TUSCAN, DORIC, IONIC, IONIC
MODERN, CORINTHIAN, COMPOSITE.
1761

gree and in the system of Masonry. It further connects the five steps to the five orders of architecture, which come from the master Architect himself, Marcus Vitruvius Pollio.

Most notably a Roman architect, Vitruvius was an engineer and philosopher who is said to have been a praefectus fabrum (officer in charge of fabrication) or praefect architectus armamentarius (architect of armaments or weapons) in service to the Roman military. The prominent orders that Vitruvius delineated is well known today in his surviving work *De Architectura Libri Deccum*, or known in the west as *Ten Books of Architecture*. In that work, he lays out the five orders as Tuscan, Doric, Ionic, Corinthian, and Composite - which in series relates to a history of architectural style of columns. In his ancient work, Vitruvius set the Renaissance standard of classical (reborn Neo-classical) architecture which became the proportional standard still employed in structures today. In the Rite degree, the orders of architecture are suggested to be parallels with the five senses - hearing, seeing, feeling, tasting, and smelling, from which the first three are given greatest importance as they facilitate the identification of one mason to another which was, in antiquity, an important matter when secrecy was a matter of necessity. The degree reads "Hearing, to hear the word, Seeing, to see the sign, and Feeling, to feel the grip, thus enabling one Brother to distinguish another in the darkness as well as the light."[24]

Taken together, we can see these various elements thusly:

Architecture	Sense	Relationship	Correspondance
Tuscan	Hearing	Word	Knowing
Doric	Seeing	Sign	Honesty
Ionic	Smelling	Sense	Perception
Corinthian	Feeling	Grip	Prudence
Composite	Tasting	Understanding	Wisdom

Agrippa, the great Renaissance mystic and physician, addresses the five senses and their relevancy is the pursuit of the divine names of God, as expressed in the letters of the Latin spelling of Jesus - *Ihesu*. In his work, *Three Books of Occult Philosophy*, Agrippa says, "There be five senses in man: sight, hearing, smelling, tasting, and touching... five powers of the soul... five fingers of the hand, five wandering planets in the heavens...[and] it is also called the number of the cross, yeah eminent with the principal words of Christ...hence in the time of grace the name of divine omnipotence is called upon with five letters...the ineffable name of God..."[25] This clearly puts a great importance on the five senses, yet, the degree leaves its exploration and understanding to our own further study. Before us are the practical elements of the degree and the modus operandi of its preceding segments. In our initiation, we are halfway up on our climb, with seven further steps to traverse.

Symbolic of perfection or a perfect order, sev-

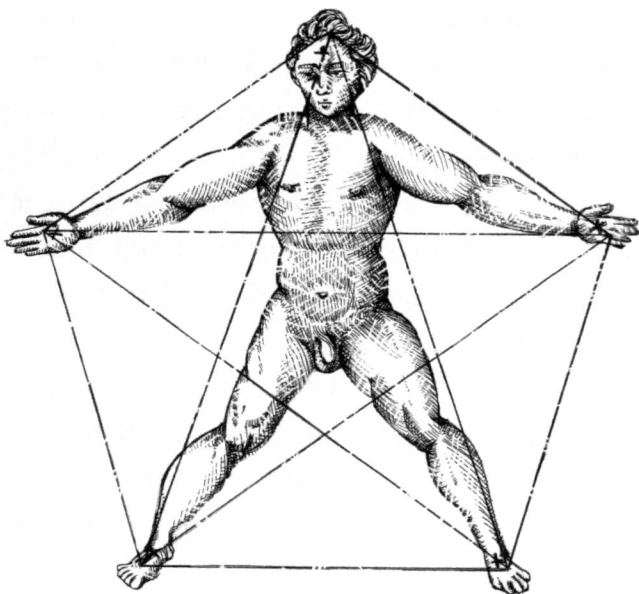

HUMAN FORM, GIORDANO BRUNO,
RECREATED FROM *ABOUT THE MONAS*
1591
GREGORY STEWART, PEN & INK ON BOARD
2016

en gives us a complete period or cycle. Cirlot, in his *Dictionary of Symbols*, suggest that seven is the union of the ternary and the quaternary endowed with the most "exceptional value."[26] This gives us an interesting aspect to explore as the ternary is suggested to represent the outcome of a third latent element from two preceding. "Unity," Cirlot says, "is split internally into three 'moments' - the active, the passive, and the union or outcomes of these two."[27] The quaternary is relatable to the physical plane in all its aspects - elementarily, hot, cold, wet, dry, etc; seasonally, in the process of physical planetary change and physically as we interpret the signs of that change around us. Cirlot, citing Jung, suggests the principal components (archetypes) of the human being are disposed similarly in quaternary order; they are: the anima, shadow, ego, and personality which all form around the idea of the God within.[28]

This ternary and quaternary give us an interesting aspect of the connection of alchemy as a spiritual development and the intersection it forms with the unification of the self and the godhead. Paracelsus, in his work *The Hermetic and Alchemical Writings*, says "Magic...had its origin in the Divine Ternary and arose from the trinity of God." God, he says, marked all creatures with this aspect of the ternary. It is when this "diffused ternary" is combined with the magical Quaternary – that, together it gives us the "whole bond" of the universe. Ternary itself comes from the Latin word ternarius which is defined to mean composed of three items. Taken in this sense, it can easily be seen as the first steps of the journey upon the stairs in our study of the number three. Quaternary, from the Latin *quaternarius*, is defined as the relation of four parts - having four sides.

Perhaps here we delve too far away from the lesson of the degree but not without purpose. In the Scottish Rite ritual, the seven steps are said to represent the seven liberal arts and sciences defined as:

- Grammar
- Rhetoric
- Logic
- Arithmetic
- Geometry
- Music
- Astronomy

The series, which can be broken into three segments are called the trivium and the quadrivium, here again our ternary and quaternary.

In antiquity, the *trivium* was composed of the educational elements of grammar, rhetoric, and logic. Those three areas of study were considered to be the scholastic key in preparation for the study of the *quadrivium* which was constituted in the study of arithmetic, geometry, music, and astrology (astronomy). Clearly, this is a very broad expanse of study and each has its unique measure of contribution to the student in both development and understanding of the physical and spiritual world around them.

In the Rite degree, great emphasis is placed

on Geometry which looks to Pythagoras who, it says, wrote above his temple door "He who knowth not Geometry is unworthy to enter here."[29] The study of Geometry, or at least the understanding of it in the material universe, is of very little importance to Masonry as no education of its meanings or teachings is provided from within its degree teachings. It is, however, re-emphasized in the Scottish Rite telling of the degree that *God* and *Geometry* are linked with the idea of Genius as illustrated with the letter "G" which is said to represent all three of these things when set within the Masonic square and Compass and in the eastern horizon of the lodge. The ritual explains saying "the blazing letter G... is the initial letter of deity (God), Genius, and Geometry. God created Genius. Genius created Geometry, and Masonry...is founded on Geometry."[30]

At this juncture, we reach an apex. With the allegorical steps of the ritual surmounted, the degree now sends the aspirant upon a series of

five allegorical voyages around the lodge representing the five ages of life and to a fellow of
the craft.

First is the voyage of mallet and chisel which
is said to be the representation of perfection of
infinite wisdom derived by the powerful instrument of the mallet. In its simplest terms this
journey represents the force of will. The chisel,
when combined with the force of the mallet as
provided by the creator, is the skill used to hone
the rude and rough state of knowledge into its
perfected shape as wisdom. Taken together, this
lesson is the adoption of will and discernment
in learning, reminiscent of the action of shaping
ones imperfect stone into the perfect ashlar.

The second journey is the lesson of the finite
and the infinite as illustrated in the symbols of
the square and compass. The square is used to
convey the idea of an unlimited expanse leading
to the infinite while the compass is used to convey the idea of a limited extent or finite measure.
Together they give us perspective to evaluate

and discern - the measure of an unending plane within the confines of a circumscribed sphere.

Third is the journey of the lever and rule which is to teach the student the power of will and action. The navigator of this journey saying, "The intelligence required in adjusting the fulcrum and arms of the lever render the lever an exceedingly appropriate symbol of weakness made strong by intellect."[31]

Fourth is the journey of the square and rule which are the symbols of regularity as a "primary distinguishing characteristic of intelligence plainly symbolized."[32] This is simplicity symbolized in the right angle created by mans own hand in the space between his outstretched index finger and extended perpendicular thumb.

Fifth is the passage of the trowel, which is the finishing step in smoothing the soft cement used to perfect the builders' work. Here we see the application of beautifying our rough work with the mud and material to smooth away and hide any material imperfections.

At last, this journey is the final lesson of the tools and brings the candidate to the end of the principal teachings of the degree. With so much information at hand, it is a challenge to approach the degree from any one particular direction and necessitates we look at its many constituent components as the whole so as to understand the degree. This is our unifying point in linking the degree to the Kabalistic path of Tav as the degree is both an ascent and descent upon this path on the allegorical tree of life. This is the action of shaping our ashlar our work on the metaphorical temple constructed within as it is our own journey of seeking personal perfection. Perhaps better said, man being made like God in the image of God - created to become creator.

But, as Tav is our first clue, it is here that we can find the parallel with the ternary and quaternary that Cirlot spoke of when we look at the Tarotic correspondence of the path. As the tarot is its own self-contained esoteric tradition, it does afford us an interesting parallel

ITERATIONS OF THE THE WORLD TAROT

of symbolic continuity in this degree with the 21st card, the World, which is in its representation, both a terrestrial consciousness as well as a universal one. Often depicted with a dancer, this visual imagery is suggestive in representing the merging of the self consciousness with the sub consciousness, the higher self with the lower, or perhaps stated as the ternary merging with the quaternary. These merged states of consciousness producing the state of being that is the manifestation of maturity at the apex of our transformation. Of the card itself, its many depictions are simplifications of broader themes. With that in mind, the traditional representation of the figure on the card is considered to be the "virgin of the world" surrounded by personifications of the four alchemical elements represented as figures of animals. Taken as a whole, the card represents the elevation from the base material into the celestial apartments of the eternal and astral universe, a juxtaposition of the states of knowledge and wisdom as they are the philosophical manifestations of learning and doing. These states become the sum of the universe, the totality of existent intelligence as it is in the physical state, no further than we may travel in our space. That is not to say that we may no longer spiritually mature or grow. But at this juncture this is our apotheosis, our apex of manifesting our whole and complete self which is our elevation above the mundane world and into higher states of consciousness.

P.F. Case, in his book *Tarot*, says of the card that whoever comes into contact with its teachings "has firsthand knowledge that he is in perfect union with the One Power which is the pivot and the source of the whole cosmos."[33] More poetically, Case says in his meditations of the tarot, *The Book of Tokens*, that "End and beginning are one."[34] Saying further,

"Though all the shifting changes of existence
I remain myself,
And the self which I am
Is thine own true self"

Echoes of this appear in Pike's writing in *Morals and Dogma* as he expounds on the Second degree. Our first glimpse of this parallel comes when Pike says "Do not lose sight...of the true object of your studies in Masonry. It is to add to your estate of wisdom, and not merely to your knowledge."[35] This could be said true of the work prescribed by the degree in that, in the seven steps, our measure of study is not simply to amass knowledge but to distill that knowledge into wisdom - from learning to doing. From wisdom comes discernment by which, as Pike says, "The true alchemist will extract the lessons of wisdom from the babblings of folly."[36] In this statement, we glimpse the underlying process at hand in becoming a Fellow of the craft which is to become a leader of society - or at least responsible to that community of fellows.

Perhaps as a testament to the idea of the second degree, Pike speaks of religion and reason when he writes "except to those who first receive it, every religion and the truth of all inspired

writings depend on human testimony and internal evidences, to be judged of by Reason and
the wise analogies of Faith...each must neces-
sarily have the right to judge of their truth from
himself, because no one can have any higher or
better right to judge than another of equal information and intelligence."[37] This is the heart
of the steps of the degree, the central purpose of
a well developed repository that develops wisdom placing us amongst equals and upon the
same level, no matter how we are circumscribed.

Going back to Cases' meditation on Tav, he
says,

"I am the end and summation of all things
The end which is without end,
Even as the beginning."

This absolutely is the idea behind Pythagoras's
vestibule sign of "Know Thyself" and the Masonic journey of a Fellow of the craft. Learning, knowledge and wisdom are forever eternal

processes that create the ever changing circum-scription of our compass.

With that realization, we can see that despite the long and many lessons in the travels of the degree, we have moved very little in space, as if climbing and descending, merging the lessons of the ideal with those of the self. This has been the journey of the path of Tav. The student has matured in the place upon which he stands, growing into his personhood - learning to BE not just BECOMING. Here before us now stands a door, but a door unlike any that have yet encountered as the now Fellow of the Craft is deep in the heart of Solomon's allegorical Temple standing before the invisible door leading to the inner sanctum, the builders' adytum that is to be the conclusion of this journey. Yet, we are a fellow of the craft, no more and no less, and as a fellow, and in this state of perfection that we forever reside with the knowledge of the tools of "being" a Mason. At our journeys start we sought light and having traversed through the pillars, ascended the stairs of existence and taken the five journeys of the fellow craft, the light we sought is our internal ignition of knowledge alchemically transformed into the cause of wisdom. This is to be our full maturation! If our blazing star was not already burning bright in the image of our maker, it has been infused with the elemental power of wisdom, in the light of knowledge. Wisdom and understanding were the lessons of Boaz and Jachin, the pillars at our entrance with their representation of the physical and cosmological universe, they are an overt testament to the breadth of the degree itself, the *Magna Matter*, which is both our physical and spiritual home in the self. Like the great patriarch Vitruvius, the fundamentals of architecture through Geometry, discovered by Genius, given to us by the creator deity in the godhead, helps us through our own personal evolution in the orders of architecture - from the rude and plain Tuscan to the complex and ornate Corinthian, this allegory illustrates our evolution. But it is in the lessons of our physical orientation that we, as fellows of the craft, are taught the lessons of the personal labor through the five journeys of our spiritual development which is a metaphor to our balance of knowledge and reason whose only outcome should be to discover the light of wisdom within ourselves. It is in this discovery of the Second Degree that we find ourselves becoming a true and permanent Fellow of the Craft.

So Mote It Be

FURTHER
LVX

And therefore what I throw off is ideal
Lowered, leavened, like a history of Freemasons,
Which bears the same relation to the real,
As Captain Parry's Voyage may do to Jason's.
The grand Arcanum's not for men to see all;
My music has some mystic diapasons;
And there is much which could not be appreciated
In any manner by the uninitiated.

BYRON'S "DON JUAN."
CANTO" XIV., STANZA XXII.

As you have advanced to this stage of the Fellow Craft degree, this work strives to impart what the symbolism hopes to inspire. These are the ideas at the heart of the degree lesson. Many are imagined and composed from other traditions - compilations of wisdom and tradition with parallel aims and expected outcomes. Many of the symbols will undoubtedly be unfamiliar, but with deeper study and contemplation, the teachings will begin to become clear. As with any Masonic work, it encourages reading of the material several times so as to open the mind's eye and see from that space between the eyes and the organ of thought.

Three Steps

To begin this study, we need first explore the work from the ritual more closely. In it, it says:

"Brother, we will pursue our journey. The next thing that attracts our attention are the winding stairs which lead to the Middle Chamber of King Solomon's Temple, consisting of three, five, and seven steps.

The first three allude to the three principal stages of human life, namely, youth, manhood, and old age. In youth, as Entered Apprentices, we ought industriously to occupy our minds in the attainment of useful knowledge; in manhood, as Fellow Crafts, we should apply our knowledge to the discharge of our respective duties to God, our neighbors, and ourselves; so that in old age, as Master Masons, we may enjoy the happy reflections consequent on a well-spent life, and die in the hope of a glorious immortality.

They also allude to the three principal supports in Masonry, namely, Wisdom, Strength and Beauty; for it is necessary that there should be wisdom to contrive, strength to support, and beauty to adorn all great and important undertakings.

Further, they allude to the three principal officers of the Lodge, viz.: Master, and Senior and Junior Wardens."

Let's pause here and consider what some of the deeper meanings infer. The first segment is fairly straightforward; the three steps allude to the three stages of human life - Youth, Manhood, and Old Age.

Youth is defined as:

(n.) Young persons, collectively.

(n.) A young person; especially, a young man.

(n.) The quality or state of being young; youthfulness; juvenility.

(n.) The part of life that succeeds to childhood; the period of existence preceding maturity or age; the whole early part of life, from childhood, or, sometimes, from infancy, to manhood.

(pl.) of Youth

This definition is a straight forward idea, especially as the degree says that "we ought industriously to occupy our minds in the attainment of useful knowledge." But how does this apply to an older initiate, someone who is no longer in his youth?

Is it a wistful thought to what was achieved when younger and in still in school? Taken on a deeper level, the idea of youth could allude to the idea of the degree itself the First degree being synonymous to mean that in the first, the candidate comes to the lodge as a youth (despite his chronological or physical age) with a clean slate of perception and a clean pallet of interpretation. The degree being his introduction from exterior life to interior life which ushers him both into the fraternity and into the concept of the undertaking. In *Morals and Dogma*, Pike calls this the focusing of the aspirants "unregulated force," the channel by which he (or she) constrain their previously raw, infantile state, into that of a youthful aspirant.

Next, the candidate enters into his Manhood, more literally the second degree, becoming a Fellow of the Craft, of which the ceremony says "we should apply our knowledge to the discharge of our respective duties to God, our neighbors, and ourselves" which is an active process to live by. We, in essence, are to achieve much by way of our doing, essentially, the work of our daily life towards our deity in worship and practice, our community in which we live and reside, but more specifically as we apply it to ourselves in continuing to apply what we've learned in our youth to this present state of existence.

The Dictionary defines Manhood as:

1. The state or time of being an adult male human.

2. The composite of qualities, such as courage, determination, and vigor, often thought to be appropriate to a man.

3. Adult males considered as a group; men.

4. The state of being human.

In the third entry, we can take much from it besides it simply being our middle state of being. It is in fact our ability to BE in the first place, our SELF in daily practice.

Interesting as this is, the second degree in which our further education takes place which makes this degree not only about the practice of our youth but also our ability to take in and apply more.

Old age is a bit more of a troubling and complex issue. So often in modern society we look at old age as a point of retirement where work and physical activity diminish. In this description, the idea of old age holds true in that the degree says of old age that in it "we may enjoy the happy reflections consequent on a well-spent life, and die in the hope of a glorious immortality" There are several interesting meanings we can take from it, especially that it is in the degree that these things take place, a literal interpretation, and that once attained, the Master Mason can live through them - literally reflecting on the life well spent. What's troubling here is that the major portion of the work of the lodge is spent in the third degree and a caution must be appreciated so as to not see the work of the Master Mason is just one of reflection and casual rest lest no work, as described in Manhood, be completed.

Old Age consists of ages nearing or surpassing the average life span of human beings, and thus the end of the human life cycle. This gives us an interesting perspective on the meaning as it implies a near end of the physical life period of time which squares with the degrees lesson as the period of reflection of a life well spent.

From this point, the degree breaks off to correlate these first steps with the three principal pillars of the lodge as Wisdom, Strength, and Beauty which also have an interesting Kabalistic point of reference in the three pillars that make up the structure of the Tree of Life.

Wisdom, the left hand pillar of mercy, which is an active pillar of the alchemical fire, and the principal of spirituality, often called the pillar of Jachin. It is a masculine pillar, and relates to our mental energy, our loving kindness, and our creative inspiration as we traverse it up the Cabalistic tree.

Strength is the left-hand pillar and takes the form of severity, shaped in the alchemical symbol of water. It can represent darkness, but it is a passive symbol that is feminine in nature. Upon it, we find the points of our thoughts and ideas, our feelings and emotions, and the physicality of our physical experience, our sensations, each an aspect of its Cabalistic progression.

Beauty, then, takes on the role of synthesis of the two, the pillar of mildness; it is upon this pillar that the novitiate is transformed through his progressive states. The central pillar of Beauty is representative of Jehovah, the Tetragrammaton which represents deity itself upon which our crown of being resides balanced through feeling and emotion from our foundation of justice and mercy, all of which springs from our link to our everyday world.

These aspects of the Kabbalah are not specific attributes of the study in the blue lodge but rather elements of deeper esoteric study, found more specifically in the degrees of the Scottish Rite. Wisdom, Strength, and Beauty are, however, specific aspects of the lower three degrees, and emphasized here in the first step into the middle chamber, so their deeper esoteric study is necessary to fully grasp their importance. As the degree instructs: Wisdom to contrive, Strength to support, and Beauty to adorn all great and important undertakings - which are the fundamentals of the three pillars in the Cabalistic study.

Conversely, as the degree states, these three pillars "allude to the three principal officers of the Lodge, viz.: Master, and Senior and Junior Wardens." and can be interpreted as such in both a micro (in lodge) fashion and in a broader macro tradition of broader connections - in this Cabalistic and alchemical way. When the alchemical aspects of wisdom and strength are combined we can see the six-pointed star of transformation appear, the symbol of transformation, often depicted in the conjoining of the square and compass, which also corresponds to the link between the Saint Johns - the Baptist as the principal of alchemical water, and the Evangelist as the symbol of alchemical fire.

From these short first few steps, we can see that there is a wealth of symbolic study at hand, but we are only one-third into our progression. Our next step takes us deeper into the middle chamber to its central position where we encounter an interesting juxtaposition of the physical world to our very human aspect of being through our senses.

For now, reflect a time on the first three steps and consider what comes next upon the path.

Five Steps Upon the Stair

The second degree holds a wealth of esoteric study and contemplation. In the preceding examination we looked at the depth and meaning of the first three steps as the conductor in *Duncan's Ritual and Monitor* ushers the candidate into the allegorical chamber of King Solomon's temple. Now, the candidate is faced with a further rise of steps, five to be exact, which is described in this text taken directly from *Duncan's*.

Stepping forward to the five steps, he continues:

"The five steps allude to the five orders of architecture and the five human senses.

The five orders of architecture are Tuscan, Doric, Ionic, Corinthian, and Composite."

From an exoteric point of view, we must look to the point of origin to the orders of architecture, which turns our attention to the grandfather of modern Architecture.

Marcus Vitruvius Pollio (born c. 80–70 BC, died after c. 15 BC) is described on as having been a Roman writer, architect and engineer (possibly praefectus fabrum during military service or praefect architectus armamentarius of the apparitor status group), active in the first century BC. By his own description, Vitruvius served as a Ballista (artilleryman), the third class of arms in the military offices. He likely served as chief of the ballista (senior officer of artillery) in charge of doctors ballistarum (artillery experts) and liberators who actually operated the machines. He has been called the world's first known engineer.

The *Vitruvian Man* illustration by Leonardo da Vinci was based on Vitrivius' proportions held in his writings. Those writings can be found in his collected works, commonly called *De Architectura Libri Decem or Vitruvius: Ten Books on Architecture*. In the work, Vitruvius describes an assortment of things from town planning to aqueducts.

It is believed that the rediscovery of Vitruvius' work had a profound influence on architects of

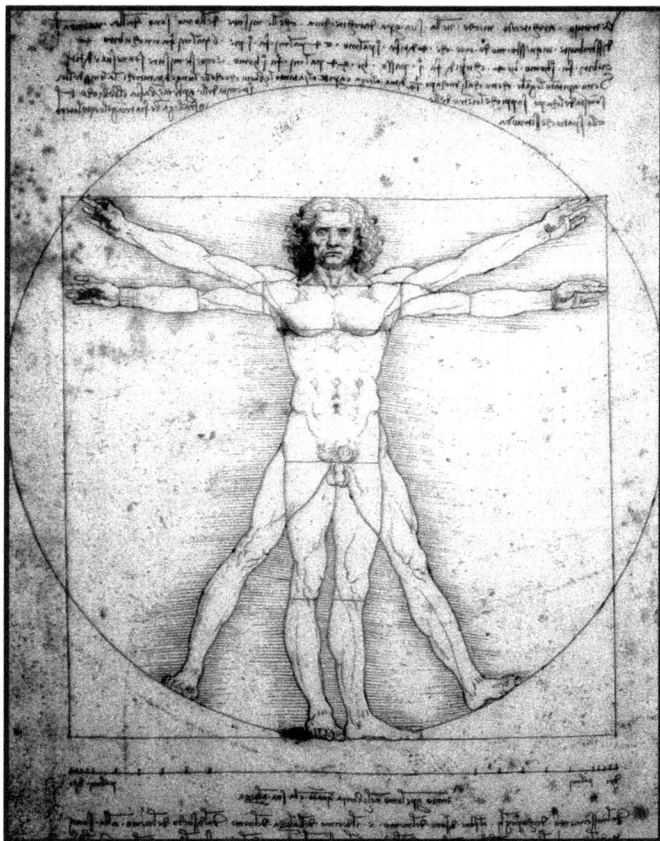

LE PROPORZIONI DEL CORPO UMANO SECONDO VITRUVIO
LEONARDO DA VINCI
1490

the Renaissance, prompting the rise of the Neo-Classical style. Renaissance architects, such as Niccoli, Brunelleschi and Leon Battista Alberti, found in *De Architectura* their rationale for raising their branch of knowledge to a scientific discipline as well as emphasizing the skills of the artisan.

Architects like Inigo Jones and Salomon de Caus were among those who first re-evaluated and implemented them as a necessary element of in their work. It was an amalgam of the arts and sciences based upon proportion and number. The architect Palladio, in the 16th century, considered Vitrivius his guide and master, making drawings based on Vitruvius' work before envisioning his own architectural concepts.

Inigo Jones, for those unfamiliar, is also the author of a Manuscript, from around 1607, on the origin of Masonry, amongst other things. Robert Lomas researches the time of Jones' Freemasonry as around 1607 when he was a surveyor to the crown under James VI.

Jones aside, the idea of Vitruvius' orders of architecture were likened to divine proportions describing in Book IV the middle three, Doric, Ionic, and Corinthian, in a celestial manner. Vitruvius writes:

"On finding that, in a man, the foot was one-sixth of the height, they applied the same principle to the column, and reared the shaft, including the capital, to a height six times its thickness at the base. Thus the Doric column, as used in buildings, began to exhibit the proportion, strength, and beauty of a man.

Just so afterwards, when they desired to construct a temple to Diana in a new style of beauty [Ionic], they translated these footprints into terms characteristic of the slenderness of women, and thus first made a column the thickness of which was only one eighth of its height, so that it might have a taller look. At the foot, they substituted the base in place of a shoe; in the capital they placed the volutes, hanging down at the right and left like curly ringlets, and or-

namented its front with cymatia and wide fes-
toons of fruit arranged in place of hair, while
they brought the flutes down the whole shaft,
falling like the folds in the robes worn by ma-
trons. Thus in the invention of the two different
kinds of columns, they borrowed manly beauty,
naked and unadorned, for the one, and for the
other the delicacy, adornment, and proportions
characteristic of women....

The third order, called Corinthian, is an imita-
tion of the slenderness of a maiden; for the out-
lines and limbs of maidens, being more slender
on account of their tender years, admit of pret-
tier effects in the way of adornment."

While not overtly esoteric in the sense of
mystic marks, his use of the human form as rep-
resentable to divine proportion does lend itself
to a Hermetic understanding of the image of
man in as a divine source, in proportion to the
temples it was used as adornment.

From an esoteric standpoint, we can begin to
infer much of how this translates to our work as

a Freemason, building that unseen house… but this also has a practical application that would have been at the very forefront of our early forbearers thought, as with Inyo Jones, as they planned and built the neo-classical temples of the Renaissance. Perhaps in some ways this is a vestige to our very being a Freemason, homage to our ancient practicing brothers.

The second degree then turns from the idea of architecture to the aspect of our human senses, five in total, linked to specific ability to hear, see, and feel. The degree says:

"The five human senses are hearing, seeing, feeling, smelling, and tasting, the first three of which have ever been highly esteemed among Masons: hearing, to hear the word; seeing, to see the sign; feeling, to feel the grip, whereby one Mason may know another in the dark as well as in the light."

Again, as the orders of architecture are of a specific physicality, so too is this treaties on the five senses. It speaks much to our physically interpreting the activity around us. In many ways it is reminiscent of the motto "Aude, Vide, Tace" which from the Latin translates to say "Know, Dare, Be Silent" which goes further to suggest the same tactile senses:

- Hearing – knowing
- Seeing – daring
- Feeling – touching in silence

The longer Roman proverb reads *"Audi, vide, tace, si tu vis vivere"* which means to "Hear, see, be silent, if you wish to live (in peace)."

This middle chamber, middle position, examination gives us much to reflect on especially as it relates to our physicality in the role of an entered apprentice.

Cornelius Agrippa, in his *Three Books of Occult Philosophy*, as we've already explored, says of the five senses:

"There be five senses in man, sight, hearing, smelling, tasting, and touching: five powers in the soul..., five fingers of the hand, five wandering planets in the heavens.... It is also called the number of the cross, yea eminent with the principal wounds of Christ, whereof he vouchsafed to keep the scars in his glorified body. The heathen philosophers did dedicate it as sacred to Mercury, esteeming the virtue of it to be so much more excellent than the number four, by how much a living thing is more excellent than a thing without life.... Hence in time of grace the name of divine omnipotence is called upon with five letters...the ineffable name of God was [expressed] with five letters Ihesu."

Clearly, we can see that Agrippa found some greater importance in the five senses, broadening their and wraps them in the vestiges of his faith. What we can take from this is that the five senses can be as limited as we choose to see them or as broad as we can interpret them to be, but that in either case, they have a vide variance by which to see them as more than just the five points of perfection.

Before us is the next ascent that take us to the point of our becoming a Fellow of the Craft.

Seven is the Magic Number

In the traditional telling of the degree, the ritual says:

"The seven steps allude to the seven Sabbatical years, seven years of famine, seven years in building the Temple, seven golden candlesticks, Seven Wonders of the World, seven wise men of the east, seven planets; but, more especially, the seven liberal arts and sciences, which are: Grammar, Rhetoric, Logic, Arithmetic, Geometry, Music and Astronomy."

Each of these arts, as they are defined, comes with a specific exoteric meaning; they are what they presume to be, in fact they are what we consider to be the liberal arts of study in university today.

But why a liberal arts course of study? Harvard University says of a liberal arts education that, "A liberal education is...a preparation for the rest of life...an education conducted in a spirit of free inquiry undertaken without concern for topical relevance or vocational utility. This

kind of learning is not only one of the enrich-
ments of existence; it is one of the achievements
of civilization. It heightens students' awareness
of the human and natural worlds they inhabit. It
makes them more reflective about their beliefs
and choices, more self-conscious and critical
of their presuppositions and motivations, more
creative in their problem-solving, more percep-
tive of the world around them, and more able
to inform themselves about the issues that arise
in their lives, personally, professionally, and so-
cially."

This is no subtle assertion; the creators of
the Masonic degrees foreshadowed that understanding included the instruction to pursue
their study in this program to better make the
Mason. In short, to make the man a better man,
one must have a firm understanding of the Liberal Arts as a necessary foundation for his being.

But what exactly does that mean? To see that
answer, we must look at what resides within the
study of the liberal arts as instructed by the tra-

ditional teaching.

Common knowledge to those who have stood in their illumination, the seven liberal arts deserve a definition as they are the core composition of what makes a Mason Free.

Grammar is the body of rules describing the properties of language. A language is such that its elements must be combined according to certain patterns generally understood by the society into which those patterns have evolved. This patterning is concerned with the morphology, the building blocks of language; and syntax, the construction of meaningful phrases, clauses and sentences with the use of morphemes and words.

The first English grammar educational tool *Pamphlet for Grammar*, by William Bullokar, was written with the goal of demonstrating that English was equally as rule-bound as Latin. Published in 1586, Bullokar's grammar was modeled on William Lily's Latin grammar, *Rudimenta Grammatices*, of 1534, which was the prescribed text used in schools in the schools of England under Henry VIII.

Grammar is simply the study, exercise and use of language in the communication of ideas to others.

Rhetoric is the art of using grammar and language to communicate effectively and persuasively. Its practice involves three key audience appeals: logos, pathos, and ethos, as well as the use of the five canons of rhetoric: invention/discovery, arrangement, style, memory, and delivery. Rhetoric is one of the three ancient arts of discourse. From ancient Greece to the late 19th century, rhetoric was a central part of Western education, training public speakers and writers to move audiences into action with convicted arguments,

Logic, with its origins from the Greek, it is the study of argumentation, the union of Grammar and Rhetoric. Used in most intellectual activities, Logic is studied, primarily, in the disciplines of philosophy, mathematics, and computer science today. Logic examines the general forms that arguments may take, which of those forms are valid, which may be fallacies, and it is a form of critical thinking. In philosophy, logic figures in most major areas of study including: epistemology, ethics, and metaphysics. In mathematics, logic is the study of valid inferences within a formal language.

When taken, applied, or studied together, these areas became known as the *Trivium* in medieval universities, meaning the three roads or three ways. Their study was in preparation of the *Quadrivium*, which are the next four liberal arts of ancient study. These four studies came from a curriculum outlined by Plato in *The Republic* (as written in the seventh book). More so, the same quadrivium was said to of come from the Pythagoreans, as Proclus (the Greek Neoplatonist philosopher) writes:

"The Pythagoreans considered all mathematical science to be divided into four parts: one half they marked off as concerned with quantity, the other half with magnitude; and each of these they posited as twofold. A quantity can be considered in regard to its character by itself or in its relation to another quantity, magnitudes as either stationary or in motion. Arithmetic, then, studies quantities as such: music the relations between quantities, geometry magnitude at rest, spherics [astronomy] magnitude inherently moving."

So then, the Quadrivium is composed of the four remaining areas.

Arithmetic, which is simple day-to-day counting through advanced science and business calculations and every variable and numerical permutation inbetween. In all aspects, it involves the study of quantity and measure, especially as the result of combining numbers. In common usage, it refers to the simpler properties when using the traditional operations of addition, subtraction, multiplication and division with smaller values of numbers.

An ancient tool, arithmetic can be dated to

FELLOW OF THE CRAFT

as early as 20,000 B.C.E. with records back to the ancient Egyptians and Babylonians of 2000 B.C.E. Continuous and historical development of contemporary arithmetic begins in the Hellenistic period of Greece with a close relationship to philosophical and mystical beliefs. This modality of counting is a factor in all human life from the accumulation of materials to the positions of the stars in the heavens above.

Geometry, as a quantification of form, comes from the Greek as earth-measurement, and is concerned with the questions of shape, size, relative positions and the properties of dimension and space. Euclid, Archimedes, Descartes, Kepler and Pythagoras are but a few of those who are a part of this 5,000-year-old art of lengths, angles, area, and volume. Much of that history can be seen in the wonders from the past.

Perhaps more relevant, advanced study of Geometry today looks not just into the dimension and space of number, but into its correlation to physics, algebra, and string theory just to name a few.

Music, the art of the muses, is an art form where the medium is sound. Common elements of music include pitch (which governs melody and harmony), rhythm (and its associated concepts tempo, meter, and articulation), dynamics and the sonic qualities of timbre and texture.

More than the study of melody and song, the Pythagoreans of ancient Greece are the first researchers to have investigated the expression of music in scale in terms of numerical ratios, particularly the ratios of small integers. Their central doctrine was that "all nature consists of harmony arising out of number," a concept still at work in contemporary composition.

Music, then, in its basic form of composition and in its deeper esoteric study, lends itself to the exploration of mathematics, logic and perhaps geometry leading to a better understanding of the universe itself.

Astronomy, the last in our quartet, this oft-maligned field was more precisely called astrology in its earliest Western study. Astrology and astronomy were archaically one and the same discipline (Latin: *astrologia*), and were only gradually recognized as separate during the age of Reason.

Since then, the two fields have come to be regarded as completely separate disciplines. Astronomy, the study of objects and phenomena originating beyond the Earth's atmosphere, as a science, is a widely-studied academic discipline. Astrology, which uses the apparent positions of celestial objects as the basis for psychological prediction of future events, and other esoteric knowledge, is less a science and typically defined as a form of divination.

Yet, in early esoteric and mystic parlance, the astronomer, despite its predictive application, would use the study of celestial bodies and their astrological movements in space and apply them to correspondences in day-to-day life. Most renaissance scientists were astrologers including John Dee, Isaac Newton, Galileo Galilei, Tyco

Brahe and Johannes Kepler.

Scoffed at in present day academia, the realm of astrology is often the fodder for cheap periodicals and psychic pitchmen. Yet, still in its deeper recesses, we can link it to the study of Kabbalah and the Western mystery tradition and find parallels to our perceptions and ideas in our symbolism. More than parlor tricks and birth signs, this field of study was at its heart a means of quantifying what would become whole fields of study under psychology and human behavior. Less sun, moon and sign and more a means to understand the nature of decisions, personality and interactions between people.

Yet, as these speak to the seven liberal arts, it says nothing of the farther correspondences mentioned at the beginning of this segment. We must turn our Masonic attention to the seven Sabbatical years, the seven years of famine, the seven years in building the Temple, the seven golden candlesticks, the Seven Wonders of the World, the seven wise men of the east, and the seven planets. Briefly, I wanted to touch on what each of those allude to and see if we can find any deeper esoteric meaning.

The seven Sabbatical years, known also as *Shmita*, refers to the seventh year of a seven-year agricultural cycle as mandated by the Torah for the Land of Israel. During that year, the land is to lie fallow and all agricultural activity is to cease. This telling comes to us from the book of *Leviticus* which makes promise of bountiful harvests to those who are observant.

The seven years of famine stems, literally, from *Genesis 41:30* which reads "And there shall arise after them seven years of famine; and all the plenty shall be forgotten in the land of Egypt; and the famine shall consume the land" which follows a seven-year period of great abundance.

The seven years in building the Temple clearly pertains to the story of Solomon building the temple in which "...King Solomon raised up a labor force out of all Israel - and the labor force was thirty thousand men...Solomon selected seventy thousand men to bear burdens, eighty thousand to quarry stone in the mountains, and three thousand six hundred to oversee them." (*1 Kings 5:13; 2 Chronicles 2:2*). An effort whose work took seven years to complete. This is an interesting metaphor to the length of time in building a Master Mason.

The seven golden candlesticks, literally from *Revelations 1:20 (NIV)* which reads "The mystery of the seven stars that you saw in my right hand and of the seven golden lamp stands is this: The seven stars are the angels of the seven churches, and the seven lamp stands are the seven churches."

This could, interpretively, be seen as the Menorah which is a seven branched candelabrum used in the ancient Tabernacle of Moses in the wilderness, not to be confused with the nine branched Menorah in use at Hanukkah. The Great architect himself instructing Moses on the construction of the lamp stand in Exodus 25:31-40 a depiction of which can be found on the arch of Titus, which is a first century Roman honorific on the Via Sacra in Rome showing the spoils from Roman sacking of Jerusalem.

In both instances, these luminaries are illustrative of light as bastions in the sea of darkness.

The seven wonders of the world are very straight forward and are reflections on the impressive work of the stone masons (literal stone cutters) who came before the present-day lodge. The Ancient Wonders were (at one point):

- The Great Pyramid of Giza from 2584-2561 BC in Egypt.
- The Hanging Gardens of Babylon from around 600 BC in Iraq.
- The statue of Zeus at Olympia from 466-456 BC (Temple) 435 BC (Statue) in Greece.
- The Temple of Artemis at Ephesus circa 550 BC in Turkey.
- The Mausoleum of Halicarnassus 351 BC (to which the modern AASR SJ is modeled after) in Carians, Persians, Greeks.
- The Colossus of Rhodes from 292-280 BC

in Greece.

• The Lighthouse of Alexandria circa 280 BC in Hellenistic Egypt, Greece.

The seven wise men of the east were early 6th century BCE philosophers, statesmen and law-givers who were renowned in the following centuries for their wisdom. The title of Seven Wise Men (or Seven Sages) a title given by ancient Greek tradition.

Each of these Sages were said to represent the worldly aspect of wisdom, though each has varied a few of the more common include:

1. Cleobulus of Lindos: He would say that "Moderation is the best thing." He governed as tyrant of Lindos, in the Greek island of Rhodes.

2. Solon of Athens: He said "Keep everything with moderation." Solon was a famous legislator and social reformer, enforcing the laws that shaped Athenian democracy.

3. Chilon of Sparta: Author of the aphorism

"You should never desire the impossible." Chilon was a Spartan politician to whom the militarization of the Spartan society is attributed.

4. Bias of Priene: "Most men are simply bad." Bias was a a famous legislator renowned for his own sense of goodness.

5. Thales of Miletus: Perhaps best remembered as famously coining the aphromism "Know thyself," a sentence so famous it was engraved on the front façade of the Oracle of Apollo in Delphos. Thales was a philosopher and mathematician.

6. Pittacus of Mytilene: Governor of Mytilene along with Myrsilus, he reduced the power of nobility governing with the support of popular classes, to whom he favored. He famously said "You should know which opportunities to choose."

7. Periander of Corinth: The tyrant of Corinth. Under his rule the city knew a golden age of unprecedented prosperity

and stability. He was known for "Be far-sighted with everything."

The seven planets, from classical astronomy included the Sun and Moon and the five non-earth planets of our solar system. These were the planets closest to the sun and visible without a telescope including Mercury, Venus, Mars, Jupiter, and Saturn. They were considered wandering stars, *asteres planetai*, as they were in early times seen as non fixed objects in the night sky.

The astute observer may notice the inclusion of the Sun and the Moon as these two objects relate to the leadership of the lodge, the pillars of wisdom, strength, and beauty, and the art of the Cabala.

Of note, the early seven planets were the source of the names of the week, and in alchemy, the seven metals of the classical world: gold, silver, mercury, copper, iron, tin, and lead. Such was the importance of these celestial bodies.

Here we have reached the top of the allegorical stairs yet again in this short work. As this is supplemental information, it is assumed that the candidate would have knowledge of these things esoteric; in the sense that few would have studied them and even fewer committed what they learned to memory. And, that the candidate would seek out this information to educate and enlighten himself as to what these deeper meanings represent. Clearly, the second degree is a wealth of information, from the suggestion of the pillars of Wisdom, Strength, and Beauty as a conduit to the study of the Cabala, to the study of alchemy in its assertion of the significance of the seven planets and what we can infer from them. The obvious statement is that there is much more to this than what rests at its surface.

CHANGE
FROM WITHIN

Except to those who first receive it, every religion and the truth of
all inspired writings depend on human testimony and
internal evidences, to be judged of by Reason and
the wise analogies of Faith.

ALBERT PIKE, MORALS AND DOGMA, 1871

One of the overt lessons of the Fellow Craft degree is that of change. Both in its mechanical process and so too in it more subtle psychological development.

This desire for change has become evident in the past 100 years on many fronts. The need for government, corporate, and school reform and even reform in the way the family system operates have all come under scrutiny and been changed as a result. This sort of holistic reformation is, in part, at the core of what the Fellowcraft degree is about. But not just reform for the sake of reform, but by the steadied beat of progression in understanding of the needs to the participants and beneficiaries of the change. In many instances, this change or progress is the manifestation of Will, the execution of a greater force than the one opposing it and quite often the product of many years of institutional thinking. This system of masonry itself is a system of progressive change from what had existed in the past, dominated by many years of institution normalizing which had left the body of thought moribund and impotent. To change necessitates a will to be different, from what was the normal to something better.

How this change occurs in this degree is through the operation of learning, the direct and open resolve to learn something new and then progress in that learning to achieve something better than what was. As a degree, the Fellow of the Craft is taught the value of the seven liberal arts which are progressive and go beyond the static measure of a few short years of life learning. Instead it charges us to spend our whole life learning and applying what we discover in the worlds we inhabit and better shape the civil life around us as well as the breadth of the civil society we inhabit.

To do this, we must first journey within and identify what that means and how best to make it a component of our being.

Relevant to this journey is the path of life in our three stages of maturation and on the five orders of architecture which here are allegorical symbols of change proportioned over time. Just as our tasks in culture mature through experience, our personal change comes in our experiences and expectations of lessons of the tracing board and the message it strives to impart in its application to this degree.

SECOND DEGREE MODERN MASONIC TRACING BOARD
GREGORY STEWART, DIGITAL COLLAGE
2007

Second Degree Modern Tracing Board

In this image, you will notice several key aspects of the degree which have earlier been explored. Here now we must interpret the image and the degree overall so as to contemplate it more as a sum total equation and see it as a reflection on our own personal journey in this *Great Work*.

Between the pillars of Boaz and Jachin on the left and right, bordered by the waters of primordial chaos and the canopy of heaven, we begin our inward journey of perfection. This journey is an eternal one and concluded only in our reaching and understanding the divine through our faith practice or in the perfection of our being through the contemplative tradition we ascribe. As this is only our second step in the progress, it is one we need spend many years perfecting and renewing so as to reach a level of enlightenment and joy which comes at the end of a life well spent.

At the beginning, this comes as the life well

spent but only after the pursuit of some greater purpose of self. All who pass under the threshold of the degrees reads the message of "Know Thyself," but what does that mean? Perhaps the second degree should add to that message, "Knowledge of the self is divine" which would spur on our desire (will) to learn and continue to grow.

Ultimately, at this stage we desire growth, both in the system and in the world in general. Why else would we be seeking beyond the knowledge and tradition of the Apprentice degree and strive to do more?

For this consideration, we look to the symbol of the Hermetic Universe which gives us a visual of the Tree of Life as a vehicle by which to see our present place and to what we can aspire. As the second degree is still very low upon the allegorical branches, we can look at our work as a progress to our advancement and the early bearing of fruit from the work. While our placement is on the low realms of the divine universe, like a young sapling our limbs reach upwards to the heavens to soak in its celestial rays and its nourishment of divine light. The path of Tav is, essentially, our progressive growth upwards towards the divine reaches above, achieved in our study and acquisition of knowledge and in the application of that knowledge to the world around us.

The realm within which we stretch is the realm of air above the *Prima Materia* and the transition space of the heavens. It holds a degree of change where all things are possible and all branches are still yet traversable by our decisions. This gives us the space to contemplate how our transformation is both the reflection of the world below us and the universe above making impact of both to be the change we desire to be and to see. To be a Fellow of the Craft, we must act to create the action which is the underlying theme of our ascension which comes at the next stage of our elevation in the third degree.

Rosicrucian mythology tells us this transformation was an alchemical process in the transmutation of lead into Gold or the creation of the proverbial Philosopher's Stone. In some respects, this is the allegory to the greater transformation at hand. While modern science tells us that this process is chemically possible, the allegorical implication is a much better approbation of the truth as true Gold is not a material refinement but an inner glimpse of what is right and good. We can find parallels of this gold and the benefit of its search in Hermetica, which tells us that the only thing truly good is the divine itself and that all else is merely a manifestation to achieve that same goodness of spirit. It is a reflection of the divine maker and all that it produces to be such which is our part of this journey.

In the mission of the early Rosicrucians was the charge to go out and observe but also to benefit those in need, to heal and mend those who needed help and healing. This was the foundation of learning, seeking knowledge, and applying that knowledge so as to raise up humanity and educate it to a place of beneficence for all.

And here we find the light emitted from the Blazing Star of the divine which is, as the tracing board alludes, a light from within which is the reflection of the greater light from above. In the Hermetic texts, we are taught the lessons of the creative craftsman, and like the avatars of all faith traditions, we must strive to do the work of the *Great Architect* and strive to do good. This photonic energy comes in our application of the mysteries and our betterment which rests in the bosom of the wellbeing of all mankind. Ultimately this is the applied knowledge of the Golden Rule, the highest level of civil respect and mutual benefit for all mankind.

For now, consider your manifestation of will and your dedication to this study and the broader application of it to the world in general. Also, consider your continued enlightenment in education and how you apply that to your development as a Mason both in life and in our manifestation as a higher being. Consider what it is you learn and what it is you would like to know as you reconcile the two, bringing them together to construct the total summation of YOU. Once you've addressed these questions, consider how to achieve the change you would like to see and then follow through with the steps of betterment in seeking the internal light of you as creator.

Aspects and Techniques of Meditation

To achieve this quality of contemplation, the suthor suggests some of these meditative techniques so as to tap into that inner peace which is the voice of the Great Architect. These techniques may already parallel the vehicles by which you presently seek enlightenment, but if you do not already practice some measure of self-discovery a technique such as the one below will help you visualize the ideas in your mind's eye.

Aspects of imagery and meditation visualization techniques have existed from the earliest of times and to various ends.

Such techniques have been proven to temporarily alleviate discomfort, accelerate the healing process and reduce stress and anxiety. It also has had some consideration as prayer technique with parallels across all faith traditions.

The goal of visualization meditation is to concentrate singularly on one image or idea and allow the internal mind to make as many inferences from it as possible. Visualization techniques work well for those who find it difficult to focus on a word or a particular topic. Visual imagery is a fundamental language, a mental symbolism, as everything we do or see is processed through the mind as an image and interpreted as such.

To begin most find the greatest results by practicing it for about 15-20 minutes a day. Many find it easiest to do in bed in the morning and at night right before drifting into sleep. As you become more experienced with the technique, you will find that you will be able to do it for longer periods of time and benefit more from its practice.

Breathing is very important in this technique. As you begin, take a deep breath and count quietly and slowly to 10, exhaling to a mental count of seven.

As you begin to visualize the image of your meditation, in this instance the tracing board of the degree, if need be, glance briefly at it so as to hold the image in your minds eye.

Breathe in with the nose and out with the mouth, slowly, and begin to contemplate the various aspects of the image.

Visualize the scene within it, the symbols, and their meanings.

Contemplate the imagery and what it means to you and your work in the degree.

Allow your mind to fully consider the image and then the paths of thought that emanate from it.

As you come back to a state of awareness, spend some time reflecting on the experience and any discoveries or questions that might come to you from it.

One consideration is to record any observations in a journal noting any experiences you may of had or things you encountered so that, as you continue to practice this technique, you may gain greater insight into your inner self and create for you a broader and vivid picture of the subject to which you are meditating upon.

It is highly recommended that you practice this technique as often as you can and as deliberately as you can so as to achieve the most robust results in the long term.

Here at last we reach the conclusion of our exploration of the Fellow of the Craft.

As before, we have been introduced to the idea of the Hermetic Universe. We now take steps into its spheres with the instruction of how to best experience and interpret their teaching. As from the first degree, we entered as if through a lens, focused into a community of understanding in the manner that light is collected and focused into the beam of a laser. That journey of our entrance culminated in our necessity to ascend Jacob's ladder which we climbed in the same manner as did the angels of Jacob's dream, from the physical universe into the heavens into the spiritual dimensions which we began to glimpse in the construct of the Hermetic Spheres. While this idea is merely an approximation, an artistic attempt at understanding the abstract thought, we can further quantify this journey up the path of Tav to the acquisition of wisdom through education and experience. Like the allegorical ladder the winding staircase is our abject lesson here and illustrates our further climb into the spheres. As past tradition informs us, this was our culmination and the end of our ascent within the tradition.

And so, here we stand at the landing atop the 15 steps, knowledge in mind and our instruction taken to heart. We are still in the physical universe in the region of air between the firm earth and the stardecked canopy of heaven-ever seeking to ascend higher.

The tracing board of this degree symbolizes this journey as an inner path that strives to bring us out of our own selfishness as such. But that is a narrow conception of the universe beyond the conception of deity. This takes us far afield from our study and to an abstraction of this lesson. As above is like that which is below, we are in transit to find that proof, our next step is to establish that being of both poles and discover its purpose.

This degree is the essence of vibration, as the *Kybalion* teaches, everything vibrates with and is in resonance to those things around them. Our acquisition of knowledge matures into wisdom by application which is what our next task in this degree represents.

Congratulations on the culmination of your study and the undertaking of this *Great Work*. As you well know, all great outcomes require work, so too in this study. If you are not aware, you are gradually rewiring your understanding of yourself and of your place in the Hermetic Universe. As with the degree, you are in a state of flux, the transit station between first and third, so be receptive to the information you take in. As the degree states, "In strength shall this house be established," and therefore you are building your foundation of that house, your mansion in the heavens.

In this symbol, may we be open to the work we undertake and endeavor to work together for the betterment of mankind in both our inner and outer temple.

So Mote it Be.

READINGS ON THE FELLOW OF THE CRAFT

Because of the nature of this work, it seems an appropriate inclusion to impart herein the ideas of other more notable expounders on the nature of what it means to be a Fellow of the Craft so as to establish the substance of the history behind its study. Many have applied pen to page on the meanings of Masonry and specifically on the Craft Degrees, some with a universal effect. These are just a few short excerpts from notable past Masonic authors. As you will note, much of this scholarship is nearly 100 years or more from the past. Be that as it may, the value of these words should weigh on the heart of any individual who has been admitted through the door of the lodge.

The Meaning Of Masonry

Second or Fellow-Craft degree

by W.L. Wilmshurst

The Opening of the Second Degree presupposes an ability to open up the inner nature and consciousness to a much more advanced stage than is possible to the beginner, who in theory is supposed to undergo a long period of discipline and apprenticeship in the elementary work of self- preparation and to be able to satisfy certain tests that he has done so before being qualified for advancement to the Fellow-Craft stage of self-building.

Again that opening may be a personal work for the individual Mason or a collective work in an assembly of Fellow-Crafts and superior Masons to pass an Apprentice to Fellow-craft rank.

The title admitting the qualified Apprentice to a Fellow-Craft Lodge is one of great significance, which ordinarily passes without any observation or understanding of its propriety. It is said to denote "in plenty" and to be illustrated by an "ear of corn near to a fall of water" (which two objects are literally the meaning of the Hebrew word in question). It is desirable to observe that this is meant to be descriptive of the candidate himself, and of his own spiritual condition. It is he who is as an ear of corn planted near and nourished by a fall of water. His own spiritual growth, as achieved in the Apprentice stage, is typified by the ripening corn; the fertilizing cause of its growth being the downpouring upon his inner nature of the vivifying dew of heaven as the result of his aspiration towards the light.

The work appropriated to the Apprentice Degree is that of gaining purity and control of his grosser nature, its appetites and affections. It is symbolized by working the rough ashlar, as dug from the quarry, into due shape for building purposes. The "quarry" is the undifferentiated raw material or group-soul of humanity from which he has issued into individuated existence in this world, where his function is to convert himself into a true die or square meet for the fabric of the Temple designed by the Great Architect to be built in the Jerusalem above out of perfected human souls.

The apprentice work, which relates to the sub-dual of the sense-nature and its propensities, being achieved, the next stage is the development and control of the intellectual nature; the investigation of the "hidden paths of nature (i.e., the human psychological nature) and science" (the gnosis of self-knowledge, which, pushed to its limit, the candidate is told "leads to the throne of God Himself" and reveals the ultimate secrets of his own nature and the basic principles of intellectual as distinct from moral truth). It should be noted that the candidate is told that he is now "permitted to extend his researches" into these hidden paths. There is peril to the mentality of the candidate if this work is undertaken before the purifications of the Apprentice stage have been accomplished. Hence the permission is not accorded until that preliminary task has been done and duly tested.

The work of the Second Degree is accordingly a purely philosophical work, involving deep psychological self-analysis, experience of unusual phenomena, as the psychic faculties of the soul begin to unfold themselves, and the apprehension of abstract Truth (formerly described as mathematics). This work is altogether beyond both the mental horizon and the capacity of the average modern Mason, though in the Mysteries of antiquity the Mathesis (or mental discipline) was an outstanding feature and produced the intellectual giants of Greek philosophy. Hence it is that today the Degree is found dull, unpicturesque and unattractive, since psychic experience and intellectual principles cannot be made spectacular and dramatic.

The Ritual runs that our ancient brethren of this Degree met in the porchway of King Solomon's Temple. This is a way of saying that natural philosophy is the porchway to the attainment of Divine Wisdom; that the study of man leads to knowledge of God, by revealing to man the ultimate divinity at the base of human nature. This study or self-analysis of human nature Plato called Geometry; earth-measuring; the probing, sounding and determining the limits, proportions and potentialities of our personal organism in its physical and psychical aspects. The ordinary natural consciousness is directed outwards; perceives only outward objects; thinks only of an outward Deity separate and away from us. It can accordingly cognize only shadows, images and illusions. The science of the Mysteries directs that process must be reversed. It says: "Just as you have symbolically shut and close-tiled the door of your Lodge against all outsiders, so you must shut out all perception of outward images, all desire for external things and material welfare, and turn your consciousness and aspirations wholly inward. For the Vital and Immortal Principle - the Kingdom of Heaven - is within you; it is not to be found outside you. Like the prodigal son in the parable you have wandered away from it into a far country and lost all consciousness of it. You have come down and down, as by a spiral motion or a winding staircase, into this lower world and imperfect form of existence; coiling around you as you came increasingly thickening vestures, culminating in your outermost dense body of flesh; whilst your mentality has woven about you veil after veil of illusory notions concerning your real nature and the nature of true Life. Now the time and the impulse have at last come for you to turn back to that inward world. Therefore reverse your steps. Look no longer outwards, but inwards. Go back up that same winding staircase. It will bring you to that Centre of Life and Sanctum Sanctorum from which you have wandered."

When the Psalmist writes "Who will go up the hill of the Lord? Even he that hath clean hands and a pure heart," the meaning is identical with what is implied in the ascent of the inwardly "winding staircase" of the Second Degree. Preliminary purification of the mind is essential to it's rising to purer realms of being and loftier conscious states than it has been accustomed to. If "the secrets of nature and the principles of intellectual truth" are to become revealed to its view, as the Degree intends and promises, the mentality must not be fettered by mundane interests or subject to disturbance by carnal passions. If it is to "contemplate its own intellectual faculties and trace them from their development" until they are found to "lead to the throne of God Himself" and to be rooted in Deity, it must discard all its former thought-habits, prejudices and preconceptions, and be prepared to receive humbly the illumination that will flood into it from the Light of Divine Wisdom.

For the determined student of the mental discipline implied by the Second Degree there may be recommended two most instructive sources of information and examples of personal experience. One is the *Dialogues of Plato* and the writings of Plotinus and other Neo-Platonists. The other is the records of the classical Christian contemplatives, such as Eckhart or Ruysbroeck or the *Interior Castle* of St. Theresa. *The Phoedrus* of Plato, in particular, is an important record by an initiate of the ancient Mysteries of the psychological experiences referred to in the Fellow-Craft Degree.

The subject is too lengthy for further exposition here beyond again indicating that it is in the illumined mental condition attained in this Degree that the discovery is made of the Divine Principle at the center of our organism; and that the sign of the Degree is equivalent to a prayer that the sunlight of that exalted state may "stand still" and persist in us until we have affected the overthrow of all our "enemies" and eradicated all obstacles to our union with that Principle.

The reference to our ancient brethren receiving their wages at the porch way of the Temple of Wisdom is an allusion to an experience common to everyone in the Fellow-Craft stage of development. He learns that old scores due by him to his fellowmen must be paid off and old wrongs righted, and receives the wages of past sins recorded upon his sub consciousness by that pencil that observes and there records all our thoughts, words and actions. The candidate leading the philosophic life realizes that he is justly entitled to those wages and receives them without scruple or diffidence, knowing himself to be justly entitled to them and only too glad to expiate and purge himself of old offences. For we are all debtors to someone or other for our present position in life, and must repay what we owe to humanity--perhaps with tears or adversity--before we straighten our account with that eternal Justice with which we aspire to become allied.

The Masonic Initiation

To All Builders in the Spirit

by W. L. Wilmshurst

Let the reader reflect that Masonic "labor" involves the making of his being whole and perfect; that it is intended to "render the circle of it complete." His complete being is likened, in geometrical terms, to a circle-the symbol of wholeness, entirety, self-contentedness. But let him remember that as he knows himself at present, he is not a circle, but a square, which is but the fourth part of a circle. Where are the other three-fourths of himself - for until he knows these as well as the fourth part which he does know, he can never make the circle of his being complete, nor truly know himself.

This is the point at which Masonry becomes mystical Geometry the important science of which Plato affirmed that no one should enter the Academy where true philosophy and ontology were to be learned, until he already was well versed in that science. For in former times these deeper problems of being were the subject of geometrical expression, and echoes of the science remain to us in our references to squares, triangles and circles, and particularly in the 47th problem of the first book of Euclid, which is now the distinctive emblem of those who have won to Mastership. How many of those who now wear that emblem, one wonders, have any conception of its significance? It is a mathematical symbol representing, for those who can read it, the highest measure of human attainment in the science of reconstructing the human soul into the Divine image from which it has fallen away. No wonder the great Initiate who composed this symbol was raised to an ecstasy of joy on realizing in his own being all that it implies, depicts, and demonstrates, and that upon that fortunate occasion he "sacrificed a hecatomb of oxen"-an expression the meaning of which, like the symbol itself, must be left to the reader's reflection, for these matters cannot be summarily or superficially explained. Pythagoras himself is said to have refused to explain them to his own pupils until they had undergone five years' silence and meditation upon them. Those five years represent the period that is still theoretically allotted to the work of the Fellow-Craft Degree, in regard to which the modern Mason is instructed to devote himself to reflecting upon the secrets of nature (i.e., his own nature) and the principles of intellectual truth, until they gradually disclose themselves to his view and reveal his own affiliation to the Deity. In declining to explain these geometrical truths to students until they had familiarized themselves with them for five years, the meaning of the great teacher of Crotona was that, by that time, the earnest disciple would have discerned their import, and gone far to realize it, for himself.

Morals and Dogma

Fellow Craft

by Albert Pike

IN the Ancient Orient, all religion was more
or less a mystery and there was no divorce from
it of philosophy. The popular theology, taking
the multitude of allegories and symbols for real-
ities, degenerated into a worship of the celestial
luminaries, of imaginary Deities with human
feelings, passions, appetites, and lusts, of idols,
stones, animals, reptiles. The onion was sacred to
the Egyptians, because its different layers were
a symbol of the concentric heavenly spheres. Of
course the popular religion could not satisfy the
deeper longings and thoughts, the loftier aspirations of the Spirit, or the logic of reason. The
first, therefore, was taught to the initiated in the
Mysteries. There, also, it was taught by symbols.
The vagueness of symbolism, capable of many
interpretations, reached what the palpable and
conventional creed could not. Its indefiniteness
acknowledged the abstruseness of the subject:

it treated that mysterious subject mystically: it endeavored to illustrate what it could not explain; to excite an appropriate feeling, if it could not develop an adequate idea; and to make the image a mere subordinate conveyance for the conception, which itself never became obvious or familiar.

Thus the knowledge now imparted by books and letters, was of old conveyed by symbols; and the priests invented or perpetuated a display of rites and exhibitions, which were not only more attractive to the eye than words, but often more suggestive and more pregnant with meaning to the mind.

Masonry, successor of the Mysteries, still follows the ancient manner of teaching. Her ceremonies are like the ancient mystic shows,-- not the reading of an essay, but the opening of a problem, requiring research, and constituting philosophy the arch-expounder. Her symbols are the instruction she gives. The lectures are endeavors, often partial and one-sided, to interpret

FELLOW OF THE CRAFT

these symbols. He who would become an accomplished Mason must not be content merely to hear, or even to understand, the lectures; he must, aided by them, and they having, as it were, marked out the way for him, study, interpret, and develop these symbols for himself.

Masonry felt that this Truth had the Omnipotence of God on its side; and that neither Pope nor Potentate could overcome it. It was a truth dropped into the world's wide treasury, and forming a part of the heritage which each generation receives, enlarges, and holds in trust, and of necessity bequeaths to mankind; the personal estate of man, entailed of nature to the end of time. And Masonry early recognized it as true, that to set forth and develop a truth, or any human excellence of gift or growth, is to make greater the spiritual glory of the race; that whosoever aids the march of a Truth, and makes the thought a thing, writes in the same line with MOSES, and with Him who died upon the cross, and has an intellectual sympathy with the

Deity Himself.

The best gift we can bestow on man is manhood. It is that which Masonry is ordained of God to bestow on its votaries: not sectarianism and religious dogma; not a rudimental morality that may be found in the writings of Confucius, Zoroaster, Seneca, and the Rabbis, in the *Proverbs* and *Ecclesiastes*; not a little and cheap common-school knowledge; but manhood and science and philosophy.

Knowledge is convertible into power, and axioms into rules of utility and duty. But knowledge itself is not Power. Wisdom is Power; and her Prime Minister is JUSTICE, which is the perfected law of TRUTH. The purpose, therefore, of Education and Science is to make a man wise. If knowledge does not make him so, it is wasted, like water poured on the sands. To know the formulas of Masonry, is of as little value, by itself, as to know so many words and sentences in some barbarous African or Australasian dialect. To know even the meaning of the symbols, is but little, unless that adds to our wisdom, and also to our charity, which is to justice like one hemisphere of the brain to the other.

Do not lose sight, then, of the true object of your studies in Masonry. It is to add to your estate of wisdom, and not merely to your knowledge. A man may spend a lifetime in studying a single specialty of knowledge,--botany, conchology, or entomology, for instance,--in committing to memory names derived from the Greek, and classifying and reclassifying; and yet be no wiser than when he began. It is the great truths as to all that most concerns a man, as to his rights, interests, and duties that Masonry seeks to teach her Initiates.

The wiser a man becomes, the less will he be inclined to submit tamely to the imposition of fetters or a yoke, on his conscience or his person. For, by increase of wisdom he not only better knows his rights, but the more highly values them, and is more conscious of his worth and dignity. His pride then urges him to assert his independence. He becomes better able to assert it also; and better able to assist others or his country, when they or she stake all, even existence, upon the same assertion. But mere knowledge makes no one independent, nor fits him to be free. It often only makes him a more useful slave. Liberty is a curse to the ignorant and brutal.

The true Mason is he who labors strenuously to help his Order effect its great purposes. Not that the Order can affect them by itself; but that it, too, can help. It also is one of God's instruments. It is a Force and a Power; and shame upon it, if it did not exert itself, and, if need be, sacrifice its children in the cause of humanity, as Abraham was ready to offer up Isaac on the altar of sacrifice. It will not forget that noble allegory of Curtius leaping, all in armor, into the great yawning gulf that opened to swallow Rome. It will TRY. It shall not be its fault if the day never comes when man will no longer have to fear a conquest, an invasion, a usurpation, a rivalry of nations with the armed hand, an interruption of civilization depending on a marriage-royal, or a birth in the hereditary tyrannies; a partition of the peoples by a Congress, a dismemberment by the downfall of a dynasty, a combat of two religions, meeting head to head, like two goats of darkness on the bridge of the Infinite: When they will no longer have to fear famine, spolia- tion, prostitution from distress, misery from lack of work, and all the brigandages of chance in the forest of events: when nations will gravitate about the Truth, like stars about the light, each in its own orbit, without clashing or collision; and everywhere Freedom, cinctured with stars, crowned with the celestial splendors, and with wisdom and justice on either hand, will reign supreme.

In your studies as a Fellow-Craft you must be

guided by REASON, LOVE and FAITH.

Masonry is a march and a struggle toward the Light. For the individual as well as the nation, Light is Virtue, Manliness, Intelligence, Liberty. Tyranny over the soul or body, is darkness. The freest people, like the freest man, is always in danger of re-lapsing into servitude. Wars are almost always fatal to Republics. They create tyrants, and consolidate their power.

Let no Fellow-Craft imagine that the work of the lowly and uninfluential is not worth the doing. There is no legal limit to the possible influences of a good deed or a wise word or a generous effort. Nothing is really small. Whoever is open to the deep penetration of nature knows this. Although, indeed, no absolute satisfaction may be vouchsafed to philosophy, any more in circumscribing the cause than in limiting the effect, the man of thought and contemplation falls into unfathomable ecstasies in view of all the decompositions of forces resulting in unity. All works for all. Destruction is not annihilation, but regeneration.

The Lost Keys of Freemasonry or The Secret of Hiram Abiff

Chapter IV – The Fellow Craft

by Manly P. Hall

Life manifests not only through action on the physical plane, but through human emotion and sentiment. This is the type of energy taken up by the student when he starts his labors in the Fellow Craft. From youth with its smiling face, he passes on to the greater responsibilities of manhood.

On the second step of the temple stands a soldier dressed in shining armor, but his sword is sheathed and a book is in his hand. He is symbolic of strength, the energy of Mars, and the wonderful step in spiritual unfoldment which we know as Fellow Craft. Through each one of us course the fiery rays of human emotion, a great seething cauldron of power behind each expression of human energy. Like spirited horses chafing at the bit, like hounds eager for the chase, the emotional powers cannot be held in check, but break the walls of restraint and pour forth as fiery expressions of dynamic energy. This great principle of emotion we know as the second murderer of Hiram. Through the perversion of human emotions there comes into the world untold sorrow, which through reaction, manifests in the mental and physical bodies.

It is strange how divine powers may become perverted until each expression and urge becomes a ruffian and a murderer. The divine compassion of the gods manifests in this world of form very differently than in the realms of light. Divine compassion is energized by the same influxes as mortal passions and the lusts of earth. The spiritual light rays of Cosmos – the Fire Princes of the Dawn – which seethe and surge through the unregenerate man, are the impulses which he perverts to murder and hate. The ceaseless power of Chaos, the seething pinwheel spirals of perpetual motion, whose majestic cadences are the music of the spheres, are energized by the same great power that man uses to destroy the highest and best. The same mystic power that keeps the planets in their orbits around the solar body, the same energy that keeps each electron spinning and whirling, the same energy that is building the temple of God, is now a merciless slave-driver which , un-mastered and uncurbed, strikes the Compassionate One and sends him reeling backward into the darkness of his prison. Man does not listen to that little voice which speaks to him in ever loving, ever sorrowful tones. This voice speaks of the peace accompanying the constructive application of energy which he must chain if he would master the powers of creation. How long will it take King Hiram of Tyre, the warrior on the second step, symbolic of the Fellow Craft of the Cosmic Lodge, to teach mankind the lessons of self-mastery? The teacher can do it only as he daily depicts the miseries which are the result of uncurbed appetites. The strength of man was not given to be used destructively but that he might build a temple worthy to be the dwelling place of the Great Architect of the universe. God is glorifying himself through the individualized portions of himself, and is slowly teaching these individualized portions to understand and glorify the whole.

The day has come when Fellow Craftsmen must know and apply their knowledge. The lost key to their grade is the mastery of emotion, which places the energy of the universe at their disposal. Man can only expect to be entrusted with great power by proving his ability to use it constructively and selflessly. When the Mason learns that the key to the warrior on the block is the proper application of the dynamo of living power, he has learned the mystery of his Craft. The seething energies of Lucifer are in his hands and before he may step onward and upward, he must prove his ability to properly apply energy. He must follow in the footsteps of his forefather, Tubal-Cain, who with the mighty strength of the war god hammered his sword into a plowshare. Incessant vigilance over thought, action, and desire is indispensable to those who wish to make progress in the unfolding of their own being, and the Fellow Craft's degree is the degree of transmutation. The hand that slays must lift the fallen, while the lips given to cursing must be taught to pray. The heart that hates must learn the mystery of compassion, as the result of a deeper and more perfect understanding of man's relation to his brother. The firm, kind hand of spirit must curb the flaming powers of emotion with an iron grip. In the realization and application of these principles lies the key of the Fellow Craft.

In this degree, the two points of the compass (one higher than the other), symbolize the heart and mind, and with the expression of the higher emotions the heart point of the compass is liberated from the square, which is an instrument used to measure the block of matter and therefore symbolizes form.

A large percentage of the people of the world at the present time are passing through, spiritually, the degree of the Fellow Craft, with its five senses. The sense perceptions come under the control of the emotional energies, therefore the development of the senses is necessary to the constructive expression of the Fellow Craft power. Man must realize that all the powers which his many years of need have earned for him have come in order that through them he may liberate more fully the prisoner within his own being. As the Fellow Craft degree is the middle of the three, the spiritual duty of each member is to reach the point of poise or balance, which is always secured between extremes. The mastery of expression is also to be found in this degree. The keywords of the Fellow Craft may be briefly defined as compassion, poise, and transmutation.

In the Fellow Craft degree is concealed the dynamo of human life. The Fellow Craft is the worker with elemental fire, which it is his duty to transmute into spiritual light. The heart is the center of his activity and it is while in this degree that the human side of the nature with its constructive emotions should be brought out and emphasized. But all of these expressions of the human heart must become transmuted into the emotionless compassion of the gods, who despite the suffering of the moment, gaze down upon mankind and see that it is good.

When the candidate feels that he has reached a point where he is able to manifest every energizing current and fire-flame in a constructive, balanced manner and has spiritually lifted the heart sentiments of the mystic out of the cube of matter, he may then expect that the degree of Master Mason is not far off, and so may look forward eagerly to the time of his spiritual ordination into the higher degree. He should now study himself and realize that he cannot receive promotion into the spiritual lodge until his heart is attuned to a superior, spiritual influx from the causal planes of consciousness.

Some Deeper Aspects of Masonic Symbolism
by A.E. Waite

In the Fellowcraft, it is as if the mind were to be renewed, for the prosecution of research into the hidden mysteries of nature, science, and art. But in the sublime Degree of Master Mason it is in order that he may enter fully into the mystery of death and of that which follows thereafter, being the great mystery of the Raising. The three technical and official words corresponding to the successive experiences are Entered, Passed, and Raised, their Craft-equivalents being Apprentice, Craftsman and Master- or he who has undertaken to acquire the symbolical and spiritualized art of building the house of another life; he who has passed therein to a certain point of proficiency, and in fine, he who has attained the whole mystery. If I may use for a moment the imagery of Francis Bacon, Lord Verulam, he has learned how to effectuate in his own personality "a new birth in time," to wear a new body of desire, intention and purpose; he has fitted to that body a new mind, and other objects of research. In fine, he has been taught how to lay it aside, and yet again he has been taught how to take it up after a different manner, in the midst of a very strange symbolism.

IMPERFECT SYMBOLISM

Now, it may be observed that in delineating these intimations of our symbolism, I seem already to have departed from the mystery of building with which I opened the conference; but I have, been actually considering various sidelights thereon. It may be understood, further, that I am not claiming to deal with a symbolism that is perfect in all its pats, however honorable it may be otherwise to the builder. In the course of such researches as I have been enabled to make into the Instituted Mysteries of different ages and countries, I have never met with one which was in entire harmony with itself. We must be content with what we have, just as it is necessary to tolerate the peculiar conventions of language under which the Craft Degrees have passed into expression, artificial and sometimes common-place as they are. Will you observe once again at this stage how it is only in the first Degree that the Candidate is instructed to build upon his own part a superstructure which is somehow himself? This symbolism is lost completely in the ceremony of the Fellowcraft Degree, which, roughly speaking, is something of a Degree of Life; the symbols being more especially those of conduct and purpose, while in the Third Degree, they speak of direct relations between man and his Creator, giving intimation of judgment to come.

The Symbolism of Freemasonry: Illustrating and Explaining Its Science and Philosophy, Its Legends, Myths and Symbols.

by Albert G. Mackey, M.D.

Although the legend of the Winding Stairs forms an important tradition of Ancient Craft Masonry, the only allusion to it in Scripture is to be found in a single verse in the sixth chapter of the First Book of *Kings*, and is in these words: "The door for the middle chamber was in the right side of the house; and they went up with winding stairs into the middle chamber, and out of the middle into the third." Out of this slender material has been constructed an allegory, which, if properly considered in its symbolical relations, will be found to be of surpassing beauty. But it is only as a symbol that we can regard this whole tradition; for the historical facts and the architectural details alike forbid us for a moment to suppose that the legend, as it is rehearsed in the second degree of Masonry, is anything more than a magnificent philosophical myth.

Let us inquire into the true design of this legend, and learn the lesson of symbolism which it is intended to teach. In the investigation of the true meaning of every Masonic symbol and allegory, we must be governed by the single principle that the whole design of Freemasonry as a speculative science is the investigation of divine truth. To this great object everything is subsidiary. The Mason is, from the moment of his initiation as an Entered Apprentice, to the time at which he receives the full fruition of Masonic light, an investigator--a laborer in the quarry and the temple--whose reward is to be Truth. All the ceremonies and traditions of the order tend to this ultimate design. Is there light to be asked for? It is the intellectual light of wisdom and truth. Is there a word to be sought? That word is the symbol of truth. Is there a loss of something that had been promised? That loss is typical of the failure of man, in the infirmity of his nature, to discover divine truth. Is there a substitute to be appointed for that loss? It is an allegory which teaches us that in this world man can only approximate to the full conception of truth.

Hence there is in Speculative Masonry always a progress, symbolized by its peculiar ceremonies of initiation. There is an advancement from a lower to a higher state--from darkness to light--from death to life--from error to truth. The candidate is always ascending; he is never stationary; he never goes back, but each step he takes brings him to some new mental illumination--to the knowledge of some more elevated doctrine. The teaching of the Divine Master is, in respect to this continual progress, the teaching of Masonry--"No man having put his hand to the plough, and looking back, is fit for the kingdom of heaven." And similar to this is the precept of Pythagoras: "When travelling, turn not back, for if you do the Furies will accompany you."

The Middle Chamber is therefore symbolic of this life, where the symbol only of the word can be given, where the truth is to be reached by approximation only, and yet where we are to learn that that truth will consist in a perfect knowledge of the G.A.O.T.U. This is the reward of the inquiring Mason; in this consist the wages of a Fellow Craft; he is directed to the truth, but must travel farther and ascend still higher to attain it.

It is, then, as a symbol, and a symbol only, that we must study this beautiful legend of the Winding Stairs. If we attempt to adopt it as an historical fact, the absurdity of its details stares us in the face, and wise men will wonder at our credulity. Its inventors had no desire thus to impose upon our folly; but offering it to us as a great philosophical myth, they did not for a moment suppose that we would pass over its sublime moral teachings to accept the allegory as an historical narrative, without meaning, and wholly irreconcilable with the records of Scripture, and opposed by all the principles of probability. To suppose that eighty thousand craftsmen were weekly paid in the narrow precincts of the temple chambers, is simply to suppose an absurdity. But to believe that all this pictorial representation of an ascent by a Winding Staircase to the place where the wages of labor were to be received, was an allegory to teach us the ascent of the mind from ignorance, through all the toils of study and the difficulties of obtaining knowledge, receiving here a little and there a little, adding something to the stock of our ideas at each step, until, in the middle chamber of life, in the full fruition of manhood, the reward is attained, and the purified and elevated intellect is invested with the reward in the direction how to seek God and God's truth, to believe this is to believe and to know the true design of Speculative Masonry, the only design which makes it worthy of a good or a wise man's study.

FOOTNOTES

1. See the preceding work in this series Stewart, Gregory. *The Apprentice - A Treatise on the First Degree of Freemasonry*. Los Angeles: FmI, 2014. Print.

2. In the two versions, there is some debate between the two versions, Christian and Hebrew, as to whether the two are different versions of merged into one in the Christian mythology.

3. See the Talmudic book of *Ruth* in the K'tuvim.

4. A vast amount of non-Masonic consideration has been paid to the origins and sources of this name. A small measure of this work can be found here: "Topical Bible: Jachin." Topical Bible: Jachin. Web. 18 Oct. 2015. <http://biblehub.com/topical/j/jachin.htm>.

5. "Jachin and Boaz." *Jachin and Boaz*. Jewish Virtual Library - Encyclopaedia Judaica, 2008. Web. 6 Sept. 2015. <http://www.jewishvirtuallibrary.org/jsource/judaica/ejud_0002_0011_0_09825.html>.

6. "Archæology of the Cross and Crucifix - I. PRIMITIVE CRUCIFORM SIGNS." *Catholic Encyclopedia.* Appleton, 1917. Print. - "According to St. Jerome and other Fathers, as a solemn symbol of the Cross of Christ -- "Mark Thau upon the foreheads of the men that sigh"

7. Hall, Manly P. *The Secret Teachings of All Ages: An Encyclopedic Outline of Masonic, Hermetic, Qabbalistic, and Rosicrucian Symbolical Philosophy : Being an Interpretation of the Secret Teachings Concealed within the Rituals, Allegories, and Mysteries of the Ages.* Reader's ed. New York: Jeremy P. Tarcher/Penguin, 2003. Print. p.595-596

8. Regardie, Israel, and Chic Cicero. *A Garden of Pomegranates: Skrying on the Tree of Life.* 3rd Ed., ed. St. Paul: Llewellyn Pub., 1999. Print. p.88

9. Ibid p.89

10. Kircher, Athanasius. *Oedipus Aegyptiacus*

11. *A∴A∴ is the Argenteum Astrum from the skygodproject.net, website - now offline, from printed edition.*

12. Schimmel, p. 46

13. Ibid p. 51

14. Cirlot, Juan Eduardo. *A Dictionary of Symbols*. Second ed. New York: Philosophical Library, 1962. 419. Print. p 232

15. Ibid

16. *Magna Mater - Mountian Mother, the Phrygian deification of the Earth Mother. As with Greek Gaia.*

17. Ibid p. 312

18. Ritual working under the Grand Lodge of Louisiana ritual, revised 1963.

19. See DUNCAN, Malcolm C. *Duncan's Masonic Ritual and Monitor; Or, Guide to the Three Symbolic Degrees of the Ancient York Rite, Etc.* 1866. Print.

20. Ibid, 2nd degree.

21. Wikipedia - *Hieros gamos or Hierogamy (Greek "holy marriage") refers to a sexual ritual that plays out a marriage between a god and a goddess, especially when enacted in a symbolic ritual where human participants represent the deities. It is the harmonization of opposites. Magna Mater -* Latin, "Great Mother"

22. *Golden section* (golden ratio, golden mean) - Two quantities are in the golden ratio if their ratio is the same as the ratio of their sum to the larger of the two quantities.

23. Cirlot, Juan Eduardo. *A Dictionary of Symbols.* Second ed. New York: Philosophical Library, 1962. 419. Print. p 233

24. Ritual working under the Grand Lodge of Louisiana ritual, revised 1963

25. Nettesheim, Heinrich Cornelius, and Donald Tyson. *Three Books of Occult Philosophy.* St. Paul: Llewellyn, 1993. Print. p. 262.

26. Cirlot, Juan Eduardo. *A Dictionary of Symbols.* Second ed. New York: Philosophical Library, 1962. 419. Print. p.233

27. Ibid p. 336

28. Ibid p. 270

29. This is also attributed to Plato as *"Let no one ignorant of geometry enter here."* The complete quote rendered by Byzantine poet John Tzetzes in the 12th century work Chiliades as *"let no one ignorant of geometry come under my roof."* Its authenticity is questionable yet exists in the spirit of Plato's work.

30. Ritual working under the Grand Lodge of Louisiana ritual, revised 1963, 2nd degree.

31. Ibid.

32. Ibid.

33. Case, Paul Foster. *The Tarot: a Key to the Wisdom of the Ages.* Los Angeles, CA: Builders of the Adytum, Temple of Tarot and Holy Qabalah, 1990. Print. p. 208

34. Case, Paul Foster. *The Book of Tokens: 22 Meditations on the Ageless Wisdom.* Los Angeles, Calif., U.S.A.: Builders of the Adytum, 1989. Print. p.188

35. Pike, Albert. *Morals and Dogma.* --. N.Y.: Macoy Pub. & Masonic Supply, 1900. Print. p.26

36. Ibid p. 56

37. Ibid p. 29

38. Morrow, Glenn R. A Commentary on the First Book of Euclid's Elements. 1. Pbk. ed. Princeton, N.J.: Princeton UP, 1992. Print. From Google Books https://books.google.com/books?id=JZEHj2fEmqAC&dq=The+Pythagoreans+considered+all+mathematical+science+to+be+divided+into+four+parts:+one+half+they+marked+off+as+concerned+with+quantity&source=gbs_navlinks_s

INDEX

V

Vitruvian Man 94
Vitruvius, Marcus Pollio 63, 93

W

Waite, A.E. 167
Wilmshurst, W.L. 140
Wisdom 53, 59, 64, 80, 85, 89, 90, 91, 118
World, tarot card 74, 75

Y

Yahweh 49
Yesod 52
Youth 85, 86

Z

zodiac 50
Zoroastrian 56

www.ingramcontent.com/pod-product-compliance
Lightning Source LLC
Chambersburg PA
CBHW070818100426
42813CB00033B/3429/J